Gregor Gdawietz, Wolfgang Schwehr

Vic Hermans & Rainer Engler

Futsal

Technique – Tactics – Training

Sports Pedagogical Contributor: Horst Nelles, Duisburg

Meyer & Meyer Sport

Original title: Futsal: Technik-Taktik-Training
© 2009 by Meyer & Meyer Verlag

Translated by Heather Ross

Futsal
Technique – Tactics – Training
Vic Hermans/Rainer Engler
Maidenhead: Meyer & Meyer Sport (UK) Ltd., 2011
ISBN: 978-1-84126-304-5

© 2011 by Meyer & Meyer Sport (UK) Ltd.
Auckland, Beirut, Budapest, Cairo, Cape Town, Dubai, Graz, Indianapolis, Maidenhead,
Melbourne, Olten, Singapore, Tehran, Toronto
Member of the World
Sport Publishers' Association (WSPA)
www.w-s-p-a.org
Printed by: B.O.S.S Druck und Medien GmbH
ISBN: 978-1-84126-304-5
E-Mail: info@m-m-sports.com
www.m-m-sports.com

Futsal
Technique – Tactics – Training

Contents

After I finished my career in 1990 as a player, I was convinced that Futsal would have a great future. As I had just been proclaimed best player of the World Championships, I was allowed to promote the game as a FIFA instructor all over the world. I have visited all the continents in the last 20 years.

I have been National Coach of Hong Kong, Malaysia, Iran and the Netherlands and presently I am on the magnificent island of Malta.

I usually work at the final tournaments as Technical Observer for UEFA and FIFA.

The UEFA has set up a splendid competition over the last years, which is attended by almost all of the 52 European countries. However, I think that some important steps still need to be taken if we are to succeed in maximizing the global reach of Futsal.

In my opinion, we lack a qualification tournament where games will be decided by playing home and away. There is no O/21 tournament and no women's competition. Finally, and, most importantly of all, we are not an Olympic Sport.

I strongly urge UEFA and FIFA to address these issues, as well as working on development and training forms for Futsal. Everywhere I go, people ask me for exercises, training methods etc.

After I wrote my first book for FIFA, "Youth Futsal" with my Spanish colleague Javier Lozano, I received a lot of inquiries. After that I worked jointly on a Futsal book in Hungary and published this book together with Rainer Engler first in the German language.

In view of the above, we have decided to also publish this book in the English and Dutch languages.

I hope that this book will inspire you and your players to raise training sessions, which are very necessary for developing Futsal, to a higher level.

Vic Hermans

1 What is Futsal?

1.1 No more walls!

Futsal is a variation of indoor soccer, but not just any old variation, the official FIFA and UEFA variation, the version of indoor soccer that has taken the whole world by storm. There are many reasons for the worldwide popularity of Futsal. Firstly there is the lack of walls or boards that completely or partially delineate the playing area. They benefit a few technically adept players and enable ice-hockey-like play. They are not a good idea for kids and school pupils who want to improve their technical proficiency. Even professional players sometimes find it difficult to control the ball on a small pitch (ideally a pitch measuring 20m x 40m (22 x 44 yd). Then there is the size of the ball, which is supposed to correspond to the size and weight of a normal soccer ball, i.e. a size 5 ball pumped to 1 bar over-pressure that rebounds on a hard indoor floor like a super ball if not kicked flat enough. This makes it really difficult to receive high and semi-high balls and makes truly attractive, fast combination passes the exception rather than the rule.

1.2 Futsal is different

Futsal, originally 'Futebol de Salão' (indoor soccer in Portuguese) is the most attractive version of indoor soccer. The pitch, the size of a basketball court, becomes the manageably-sized setting for teams of five including a goalkeeper, the stage to show off lightning fast ball technique, feint-packed dribbling, with almost no contact yet aggressive soccer action. Futsal has incredibly fast passing, and is the epitome of a team sport that still allows room for individual demonstrations of skill, tricks and feints that are relished by players and spectators alike. But of course it's more than just a fun sport; Futsal is an ideal youth and high school sport. Nowhere can the classic soccer techniques from safe passing to ball reception to goal scoring be learned as fast as in Futsal. This was scientifically proven by the University of Frankfurt at the end of 2006. And if you don't trust the science, note that world-class Brazilian players like Ronaldo and Ronaldinho played only Futsal in their youth and it was there that they learned the technical skills that they were later able to deploy on the full-size pitch. This is not surprising as Futsal is part of the basic school curriculum in Brazil.

"I learnt my technical skills in Futsal," said the soccer star Juninho. "Futsal requires split-second decisions, fast attacking with few players and good positioning, as well as being very physically demanding. Every player who started out playing Futsal is one step ahead of the game. " Futsal is also one of the fairest team sports; the founders of the FIFA rules have combined sensible indoor soccer rules with proven ideas from other sports, which not only speed up the game but above all minimize the risk of injury to players.

1.3   The ball is still round

So, what's so different about Futsal compared to indoor soccer with boards? Quite simply: the ball. It is quite different from the conventional soccer ball designed for the full-sized pitch and also the 'indoor soccer' ball, which is usually covered in nylon or smooth synthetic velour.

The Futsal ball was especially developed for the official FIFA version of indoor soccer and has less bounce than a conventional soccer ball. If it is dropped from a height of 2 m (2 yd), it only bounces gently two or three times and then comes to a stop. A conventional outdoor soccer ball would bounce like a rubber ball on the indoor floor surface. The reduced bounce of the Futsal ball makes it much easier to control on the hard indoor pitch surface and is therefore conducive to attractive, technically skilful soccer.

The ball is either made of leather or another high-quality material. The long-time supplier and partner of the Brazilian national Futsal team, DalPonte, manufactures its top-of-the-range Futsal ball from microfiber. Other high-profile manufacturers like Nike or Puma also offer excellent Futsal balls. For a long time, the original Puma Futsal ball was the official ball of the Spanish National Futsal League, the best league in the world.

All Futsal balls have the same size, weight and pressure. The circumference of the ball should measure between 62 and 64 cm (20-21 inches). At the start of the match it must weigh at least 400 g (14.1 oz) but not more than 440 g (15.5 oz). When pumped up, the pressure should measure between 0.4 and 0.6 atmospheres (400-600 g/cm^2). The ball should not break due to match wear and tear unless it is intentionally destroyed. It should retain its fantastic properties for a long time without significant signs of wear and tear. Its reduced bounce and small size make it ideally suited for technically less-skilled children and young people in schools and clubs.

The fact that this ball lends itself perfectly to the celebration of soccer was demonstrated conclusively by Nike in February 2006. The firm started a campaign in Berlin, Germany, with a massive 3 v 3 tournament, which focused on attractive soccer instead of aggressive or boring tactics. The name of the campaign was "Nike Joga Bonito Futsal" (Nike plays attractive soccer – in Portuguese). Brazil is now not the only place where attractive Futsal is played!

1.4 The rules promote fair play

Unlike traditional indoor soccer, the Futsal pitch is a standard size, i.e. exactly the same dimensions as a basketball court at 20m (22 yd) wide by 40 m (42 yd) long. The great advantage of this is that the pitch is already marked out on the floor of any sports hall. The goal dimensions are 2m (2.2 yd) by 3m (3.3 yd).

Also unlike traditional indoor soccer, the pitch is not partially or completely walled; the external boundary is just a line. If the ball goes outside this line, the ball is not thrown or rolled in but kicked in.

But what is it that makes the game of Futsal so incredibly fast? Take these three sample rules for starters:

1. The goalkeeper may only be passed to in his own half by his four teammates under certain conditions, thus precluding tactical, boring passing back and forth in front of the goal.

2. The playing time of 2 x 20 minutes per half is net playing time. As in handball, basketball or ice hockey, the timing is halted every time play is stopped, thus eliminating unattractive playing for time.

3. Set plays must be performed within. 4 seconds; otherwise the opposing team gains possession of the ball, so that the whole game is dynamic and fast.

Why is it that injuries are so rare in the sport of Futsal? Maybe these two example rules can give us a clue:

1. Piling into an opponent from the side or from behind is absolutely forbidden for as long as the opponent is in possession of or passing the ball, which significantly reduces the risk of injury.

2. Whereas in conventional soccer only the perpetrator is punished for fouling, in Futsal, individual fouls can hurt the whole team, as the fouls of all the players on a team are accumulated. From the sixth team foul per half there is a 10 m (11 yd) penalty kick, even if the foul began in the opponent's half. And such a penalty kick is almost always converted, which makes every player strive for fair play at all times, thus protecting particularly the technically skilled and fast players. But Futsal is not a completely non-physical sport as it is characterized by its aggression and intensity, although in Futsal, aggression is no compensation for technical weakness.

1.5   The advantages are clear

The advantages of Futsal over indoor soccer played with walls should by now be obvious.
- Futsal is a fast, dynamic game played on a small pitch.
- Futsal is an attractive, highly skilled game.
- Futsal is a high-scoring game suitable for players of all abilities.

- Futsal is an ideal introduction to the game of soccer to learn basic soccer techniques.
- Futsal is an aggressive but fair game with a low risk of injury.
- Futsal can be played according to official FIFA rules in almost any sports hall.

Many clubs discovered the excitement of Futsal long ago. And also clubs who initially struggled are increasingly changing from a rubber ball to a Futsal ball, from banging away at walls to the controlled, fast game with touchlines. Internationally, indoor soccer has been heading in the right direction for years. FIFA and UEFA manage Futsal as second only to conventional outdoor soccer. Nations like Brazil, Spain, Argentina, Russia and the USA are leading the way.

2   How to Plan Training Sessions

2.1   How to structure training sessions

The classical training session is divided into three sections:

* Introduction and warm-up
* Main section, with technical and tactical content and match-specific situations
* Final cool down

Introduction and warm-up

The first section of the session consists of simple but multi-faceted drills or game forms, which warm up the main muscle groups to be used during the main section of the session. The aim is to activate these muscle groups, the cardiovascular system and the metabolism and to raise the body temperature. The training load should gradually be increased from a low to a medium level; the players should not approach a state of exhaustion. These reserves must be preserved until the main section of the workout, when the players must have sufficient concentration and strength to be able to learn and implement technical and tactical tasks.

The exercises chosen for the warm-up must be relevant to the main section of the session that follows, and the training condition of the players must also be taken into account, not least for the purposes of injury prevention and the creation of optimal motivation.

In order to also engage the players cognitively in the learning process, they must be informed of the goals and tasks at the start of the session. This makes the players more willing to learn as they are clear about what is expected of them and it is naturally motivating to accomplish goals.

The appropriate stimulation of the nervous system leads to a mindset that promotes concentration and motivation. Special, situation-specific movement sequences should therefore be prepared.

After this first section of the session, the players should be optimally prepared both physically and mentally for the main section.

The first section can also be sub-divided into three phases that can be described as follows:

1st **phase:** activation of the cardiovascular system to improve blood flow (about 35% of total warm-up).
2nd **phase:** activation of the main muscle groups by light strengthening, stretching and loosening exercises (55%).
3rd **phase:** preparation of the nervous system and the sensory organs to cope with the coordination and speed demands of the main section (10%).

Main Section with Technical and Tactical Content and Match-specific Situations

The main section of the workout is all about accomplishing specific goals on a certain day within the context of the whole training plan. The priority is the development of physical skills and the learning and ingraining of movement sequences and techniques. Technique is improved by means of targeted drills, and a focus on tactics improves players' understanding of the game (should be age-appropriate). The training load is significantly increased and can even approach maximal levels. The players should be allowed a partial or complete recovery between the individual activities, depending on the training goal. The higher the training load, the more important is an adequate recovery.

Technique training, speed and speed strength drills should be performed during the main section as players still possess the required high concentration and neuronal resilience.

Towards the end of the main section, when concentration is starting to flag, training content should be simple and familiar, but can still include match and strength endurance.

Cool down to finish

The muscle groups prepared during the warm-up and most solicited during the main section must also receive special attention during the final third section. The training load must be reduced and a recovery process introduced. Activities should be performed at low to very low intensity that bring the pulse rate back to normal and promote the players' oxygen supply. Stretching exercises ensure a quick recovery for all solicited parts of the body.

Children and youngsters should not perform any further technique drills in the final section of the workout, as a fatigued neuromuscular system prevents the correct performance and learning of movements. Technical elements should therefore always be performed either at the end of the warm-up or the beginning of the main section.

It is perfectly acceptable for adults to perform different versions of the drills when fresh and when tired, as this reflects the different phases of a match.

2.2   Training session setting

For a training session to be carried out successfully, the coach must first ensure that the setting is appropriate. He must, for example, know how many players will be taking part, which facilities are available in the sports hall and what equipment can be used in the workout.

The optimal number of players for a training session is twelve. A higher number would mean that the coach has to concentrate on ensuring that the activity is performed than on a qualitative evaluation of the players' performance. Depending on the size of the sports hall and the equipment available, a larger group would also reduce the intensity of the drills and the effectiveness of the training time.

The coach should also subtract from the total training time the time needed for explanations, for setting up the drills and activities (equipment, forming groups, taking up starting positions, etc.) and recovery breaks and time for drinks.

Particularly in the case of young players, the coach should always try to make the most effective use of the training time.

On the other hand, with a smaller number of players, many drills cannot be performed correctly, particularly those that are intended to simulate match situations or which involve the study of tactics. In a smaller group, the training load could also exceed an acceptable intensity.

However, should the optimal group size of twelve players not be possible, the coach will be required to demonstrate his creativity and flexibility. He must make the best of the situation, e.g. by using variants, lengthening/shortening drink/recovery breaks or by differentiating within the group according to ability.

The duration of the training session depends on many factors. Firstly, and something that is usually out of the coach's control, is the time that the sports hall is available. Other sports (e.g. basketball) may take precedence and training may have to take place in less popular slots.

Once the setting has been correctly organized, the duration and frequency of training sessions naturally depend on the age and ability of the group. On average, a good starting point would be 1-2 workouts a week, lasting between 1 and 2 hours.

This is also a good point to mention that the structure of Futsal training sessions largely resembles that of conventional soccer, and very many drills and game forms from classical soccer can of course be adapted for use in Futsal training.

3 Futsal – Basic Techniques

The purpose of teaching basic techniques is to improve players' ability to control the ball on the ground and in the air in more than two touches. Technique allows the player to gain possession of the ball, to overcome one or more opponents and to support the actions and movements of his teammates.

The player must be able to control the ball, not the other way around. His skill must always serve the team and not just be used to show off. The aim is therefore to acquire the general ability to carry out a targeted technical action.

3.1 Ball reception

The speed of the Futsal ball requires that the player receives it correctly and brings it into the correct playing position as quickly as possible.

The most used technique is therefore oriented control (ball reception).

This means that the player controls and passes the balls with a single contact, using the most suitable part of his body.

Apart from oriented control, which is the most dynamic option, there are three other types of control.

- The *Stop*: the ball no longer moves

The player waits for the ball

He raises his slightly cocked foot

He stops the ball with the sole of the foot

- The *Half Stop*: the ball doesn't come to a complete stop

The player receives the ball with the sole of the foot

He pulls it to the side

And then dribbles off with it straight away

- *Dampening*: the speed of the ball is reduced as the contact surface is pulled back.

The ball drops

The player's foot moves towards the ball

He breaks the ball's flight by bringing the ball downwards at the same time as he touches it with his foot

He then controls the ball

The different ball control techniques are shown below:

Ball reception with the instep
Using a stable contact surface

The ball comes toward the player

The player pulls his foot back slightly and controls the ball with the instep

Ball reception with the outside of the foot
Used to deceive the opponent

The ball comes toward the player

The player pulls his foot back slightly and controls the ball with the outside of the foot

Ball reception with the chest
Used for balls reaching the player at chest height

| The player waits for the ball with an open body stance | He places his chest underneath the ball | He dampens the speed of the ball by lowering his chest | The player controls the slowed down ball |

Ball reception with the head
Used for high balls. Not used often, as the hard contact surface makes it difficult to control the ball and requires very good coordination.

| The player stands underneath the ball | He keeps his eyes on the ball and it lands on his forehead | The player controls the slowed down ball |

Ball reception with the thigh

Used when the ball reaches the player below chest height. The thigh has a large contact surface.

The player brings his thigh toward the ball

The ball touches his thigh and his thigh dampens the speed of the ball

The ball drops to the ground under control and is passed by the player

3.2   Dribbling and ball control

Dribbling means the technique that allows the player to move with the ball in a particular direction without the ball being taken from him by an opponent.

The following qualities are necessary for successful dribbling:
* Creativity
* Imagination
* Mobility
* Mind-body coordination
* The ability to change pace

The different dribbling methods can be classified as follows:
* *Simple:* the opponent is outplayed without any preparatory action.
* *Combined:* the player first performs a feint in order to outplay the opponent.

The different methods can also be classified according to the way in which the opponent is outplayed (one or more actions when dribbling).
* *Speed:* by suddenly accelerating or stopping.
* *Deception:* by using feints to confuse the opponent.
* *Shielding:* the ball is shielded by the player's body at all times.

When dribbling, the player uses certain techniques to move the ball along the pitch, while keeping the ball under control.

The different ways of moving the ball can be differentiated by:
* *Contact surface*
  Inside or outside of the shoe as the primary surface
  Outside of the foot and sole of the foot as important surface
  Heel and toes only in special cases

* *Speed of execution*
  Slow
  Quick

Change of pace: change pace when changing direction, alternate slow and fast paces
* *Obstacles*
  Easy (without obstacles)
  Hard (with obstacles)

The training of dribbling and moving the ball should always be accompanied by dampening and/or ball reception.

Deception

The player moves toward the defender, looks for the best position. If the opponent has an open stance, he blocks the ball then passes it through his opponent's legs, runs around him then picks up the ball again.

Shielding the ball

The player stands between the ball and the defender

and shields the ball

by moving left and right.

then he passes the ball.

Moving the ball with the heel

The player dribbles the ball

he moves his foot gently over the ball

forward

and starts dribbling again.

Moving the ball with the inside or outside of the shoe

| The player moves the ball with the inside of the left shoe. | The player moves the ball with the outside of the left shoe. | The player moves the ball with the inside of the right shoe. | The player moves the ball with the outside of the right shoe. |

3.3   Passing

Passing is vitally important in this fast-paced game. It forms, for example, the start of an attack, so accuracy is therefore paramount.

Passing is a technique and is therefore very often practiced in every training session. For correct passing (not only technically but also at the right time and to the right player), the movements of the teammates are equally as important as those of the ball carrier.

The most important types of pass are classified according to the part of the foot used:

- The *inside of the shoe* is used for short passes.
- The *forefoot* is used for longer passes.
- The *outside of the toes* is used for short, mid-length and long passes.
- The *inside of the toes* is used for mid-length and long passes.
- The *outside of the shoe* is used, for example, for short passes when the opponent is standing very close to the attacker.
- Don't forget the *lob*: this is a very important way of passing over the heads of defenders. The ball is usually trapped by other parts of the body such as the head or the chest, but if the ball falls correctly, it can also be volleyed directly by the foot.

Passing training should be done in conjunction with dribbling and ball reception.

Inside of the shoe
The player runs up to the ball

and kicks it with the inside of his shoe.

His kicking leg follows through.

Forefoot
The player's standing leg is placed next to the ball.

The kicking leg kicks the center of the ball.

The ball must be struck through the center.

Lob

The standing leg is placed next to the ball.

The foot of the kicking leg goes under the ball

and lifts the ball into the air.

Outside of the foot

The players runs up to the ball and goes to kick it.

He kicks it with the outside of the foot

and follows through with his foot.

Inside of the foot

The player kicks the ball with the inside of the foot

and follows through with his leg.

3.4   Shooting

A shot at the goal usually involves trying to score a goal after an attacking drive.

The goal shot is normally kicked by the foot, but other parts of the body can also be used.

Depending on where the foot is in relation to the ball and on the position of the player, the following different types of goalshots can be played:

- *Flat ball:* the ball is passed flat to the player and he kicks it with his foot.
- *Drop kick:* the ball is passed high and the foot kicks the ball just after it hits the ground.
- *Volley kick:* the ball is passed high and the foot kicks the ball before it touches the ground. Depending on the player's position, it is called a volley kick if the body and leg remain more or less vertical or half-volley kick if the body and leg must be bent in order to kick the ball correctly.
- There are permutations and combinations of these shots that have their own terminology, for example the *bicycle kick* (a volley kick in which the legs make a scissors movement in the air before the ball is kicked) and the *overhead kick* (a volley kick in which the whole body is off the ground and the back is facing the goal).

The parts of the foot most frequently used for shots on goal are the inside of the foot and the forefoot:

- The *inside of the foot* achieves placing and effect while the forefoot is mainly used to give power to the ball.
- The *inside of the foot* is used for precision and security.
- Use the *toes* for speed and to surprise the opponent.
- In Futsal, *heading the ball* is not as important as in 11 v 11 field soccer.

Shot at the goal with the outside of the foot

The player runs toward the ball

and kicks it with the outside of the foot.

The dropkick

The ball comes toward the player.

Immediately after the ball touches the ground,

the player volleys it.

The overhead kick

The player waits for the ball and gets into position.

The player sees the ball coming and evaluates it.

He drops to the ground and kicks the ball back behind his head

and lands on his arm or leg.

Shot at the goal with the inside of the foot
The player traps and kicks the ball

with the inside of the foot.

Inside
The player runs toward the ball,

and kicks it with the inside of the foot.

The bicycle kick
The player jumps into the air with the right leg first.

He kicks the ball with his left foot

and lands back on the ground right foot first.

The side volley
The player turns to the side to kick the approaching ball.

He kicks through the center of the ball

and his leg follows through.

Shot at the goal with the forefoot
The player points his toes downwards and kicks the ball from underneath 'with the laces'

and follows through with his leg.

Shot at the goal with the toes
The player runs toward the ball

kicks it with his toes

and follows through with his leg.

Volley shot
The player waits for the ball

and plays a volley kick with the inside of his foot.

Header
The player moves underneath the ball.

Keeping his eyes on the ball

he heads the ball with his forehead.

Jump header
The player waits for the ball, keeping his eyes on it. The player jumps, arching his back. He heads the ball with his forehead.

3.5   Feints and tricks

Feints involve deceiving an opponent by means of an action or movement that the player does not actually intend to perform. They are successful if the player's physical deception, trick or 'fakie' outplays the opponent and enables him to leave him behind. The ball carrier uses his individual skills to shake off his opponent and run into free space. If the opponent doesn't realize what is happening, he is defeated and outplayed. If the opponent does spot the feint, he can react accordingly.

A trick refers instead to a skilled maneuver with the ball that does not necessarily involve deceiving an opponent. Every Futsal player loves watching the tricks of the pros on the TV, and each one of them will have tried to copy one or more tricks at home. Often written off as a waste of time in the outdoor game, well-executed feints and tricks are always a highlight in the indoor game; they are fun for the players to perform and boost their self-confidence.

Learning feints also leads to a clear improvement in ball control, as it is impossible to perform an effective feint without it. In Futsal, it should be included in coordination training and be an integral part of the training program.

Particularly when working with children and youngsters, it is helpful for the coach to teach ball skills by means of tricks, as the successful performance of feints and tricks is motivating and pushes the players to try harder. Every player becomes very ambitious when learning feints, particularly children.

Coordination training with Futsal tricks is one of the most important parts of modern training for children and young people as it is such a great way of promoting the development of young Futsal players.

Taking the ball to the left and right

The ball carrier dribbles toward the opponent, pulls the ball inward with his left foot onto his right foot and dribbles it around the opponent with the right foot.

Passing through the legs ('Nutmeg')

The goalkeeper tries to force the offensive ball carrier away from the goal; the attacker stands between the goalkeeper and the ball and stops the ball. The goalkeeper stands with his legs apart. The player kicks the ball between the goalkeeper's legs.

Around the world

The player kicks the ball up then rotates his left leg around the ball and then traps the ball with his left foot.

Feint

The player dribbles toward his opponent, goes as if to change direction by taking his right foot over the ball. The opponent moves in the indicated direction. The ball carrier dribbles off with the left foot and passes to the left past the opponent.

Trick

The player juggles the ball and then moves slightly away from the ball, then catches the falling ball between the calf and the back of his thigh.

Playing around goalkeeper or player

The player dribbles toward the goalkeeper, pulls the ball in and lets it roll, then dribbles off using his right foot and dribbles around the goalkeeper.

3.6   Goalkeeping technique

The goalkeeper in modern Futsal is much more important than a soccer goalkeeper of even as recently as 15 years ago. His role used to be just to protect the goal, whereas the modern Futsal goalkeeper must anticipate situations and actively participate in the game. He is therefore more a goal player than 'just' a goalkeeper.

At elite level, we now frequently see goalkeepers literally playmaking. For this reason they should also perform the drills with the field players in training.

However, this section focuses only on the specific demands on the goalkeeper, not on his technical and tactical skills as a player.

The abilities a Futsal goalkeeper must possess are:
- Basic speed
- Fast reactions
- General strength
- Flexibility
- Alertness

Particularly players who start playing Futsal at a young age need to train the following basic techniques and tactics:
- Ball on the ground
- Low and mid-height balls
- High balls
- How to catch or punch the ball
- Throws
- Kicks

Goalkeeping technique

Receiving the ball
The goalkeeper moves toward the ball and bends his right knee so that it touches the ground then traps the ball with both hands.

Catching the ball
The goalkeeper must always move behind the ball. He grips the ball with both arms. The same also applies for mid-height balls.

Goal kick

The keeper waits for the ball, sets it up and then kicks it to his teammates.

Stopping the ball with the foot

The keeper reacts to the shot at the goal, stops the ball with his right foot and his left knee drops to touch the ground.

Goal throw

The keeper catches the ball and throws it with one hand to his teammates with a slight swerve.

Diving catch

The keeper reacts to the shot at the goal and pushes off his right foot. He bends his left knee and traps the ball on the ground.

Catching the ball

The keeper places his body behind the ball, and the thumbs and index fingers of both hands form a triangle behind the ball for greater control.

Punching the ball

Hold both fists together facing the ball and punch the ball with both fists at the same time.

4 Age Group Training

Age group training can be divided into the following seven categories:

- Training for 6-8 year-olds
- Training for 8-10 year-olds
- Training for 10-12 year-olds
- Training for 12-14 year-olds
- Training for 14-16 year-olds
- Training for 16-18 year-olds
- Training for over-18s (seniors)

Training emphases depend on the players' ages. Youngsters need to work on basic techniques and small-sided games and training games. Tactics and conditioning become more important as they get older.

The important thing to remember is that training for youngsters is not just a reduced version of training for adults!

This must absolutely be borne in mind when planning and executing age-appropriate training. Look inside the youngsters' world in order to better understand their wishes and ideas. Try to see things their way to make training exciting and fun for each age group.

For the sake of simplicity, the practical section features a description of age-typical developmental milestones and behaviors with corresponding consequences for training, with the emphasis clearly on training for youngsters.

No coach should neglect the fact that training for youngsters is not just about improving technical skills but also the development of their individual personalities.

To avoid overloading youngsters physically or mentally in training, which would be counter-productive for all aspects of the learning process, there are a few pedagogical principles that should always be borne in mind when working with youngsters:

- Patience!

- Allow mistakes!

- Don't aim for perfection!

Childhood is a period of physical, mental and psychological development and growth. The foundations of our adult lives are laid in these important years.

Training during these developmental years should therefore be basic and slowly built upon and should differ from adults' training in its intensity, content, structure and difficulty.

There are four general developmental phases:

1. School age – approx. ages 6-12

2. First pubertal phase – approx. ages 12-14

3. Second pubertal phase – approx. ages 14-16

4. Adolescence – transition to adulthood – approx. ages 17-19.

The fact that the boundaries between the different developmental phases are blurred is demonstrated by players aged 14-16 (first pubertal phase), when the growth spurt often leads to massive differences between players of the same age. The sudden and individual nature of these changes necessitates greater individualization of training loads.

It should therefore be noted that not only are youngsters' training needs completely different from those of adults, but also the training content and the training and game forms for youngsters should also take into account the age and development-related physical, mental and emotional differences between players.

Therefore, as mentioned above, an accurate knowledge of the individual developmental phases and their age-typical characteristics is essential for the planning and execution of an age-appropriate and successful foundation and building-up training program.

4.1 Training for 6-8 year-olds

School kids of this age still lack balance and are very sensitive; their self-confidence is very fragile. They are very quick to enthuse about new games and sports but then lose interest just as quickly if things don't go their way. If the coach is aware of this, it makes training planning and implementation much easier. An excessive training load or frequent 'defeats' in small-sided games will almost certainly put the child off the sport of Futsal for life. Positive experiences should be achievable for all participants. The prerequisite for a real positive experience is achieving something. There is a fine line between over- and under-training that requires experience and sensitivity on the part of the coach.

At this age, the child is growing fast and his slower-growing muscles often cannot keep up. This imbalance often causes ongoing movement problems that are soon overcome once muscle growth catches up.

While technique training is almost totally lacking in training for this age group, it should already include some drills that teach the gross forms of Futsal techniques. The technique drills should always be taught in a playful context and never be an end in themselves. This playful context is enjoyable and motivating for the children and makes them want to try new things.

Basic ball handling and ball control should be taught, as they are the foundation for the ongoing optimization of the game.

These include first experiences of the necessary sporting skills and abilities for Futsal. Make sure that the teaching is child-friendly. You should avoid just using a watered-down version of adult training for children. The emphasis should be on fun and play; children are not 'small adults'.

As the concentration of children of this age is limited, training sessions should not last more than one hour. It is helpful if every child has at least one ball so that the constant activity (with the ball) keeps the child attentive and 'on the ball'.

As well as the use of games that are specifically focused on improving the game of Futsal, you must also include those that promote general and all-round movement. Training games should always be relevant to the target game and match-specific. They should never contradict a desired Futsal target movement or technique.

Children need to play matches to have a genuine engagement with their sporting environment where they can experience a sense of success but also learn what it feels like to lose. Matches and 'trials of strength' should therefore be included in training. They spur on and motivate the children to push themselves. The deliberate use of appropriate games almost automatically leads to an improvement in the desired skills, partly combined with a conditioning load.

Pure conditioning training, as performed by adults, should never be inflicted on 6-8 year-olds! The improvement in conditioning should at best be viewed as a positive side-effect of coordination drills.

Successes should be praised and highlighted by the coach, mistakes, in combination with encouragement, commented on matter-of-factly. The latter should not be done in front of the group, in order to avoid adding to the child's feeling of failure in front of his friends. The role of the coach is also one of role model to the children. They often tend to be guided more by the coach than their own parents when it comes to behavior and values. The coach should not lose sight of this important fact and the responsibility it entails.

Although the aim of improving playing skills should be behind every training session, especially at this age, children should play for fun in order to lay the foundations for the long-term, or even life-long enjoyment of the sport.

Children learn by copying. It is therefore essential that the coach is able to demonstrate the drills himself.

Additional motivation is provided when the coach himself takes part in the drills as a partner or opponent. The same is also true in small-sided games and training games, for every child is proud of beating his teacher and there is the additional motivation of beating someone stronger and bigger than oneself.

As children of this age still lack an awareness of space and combinations, not too much time should be spent explaining it to them. This verbal teaching approach would only overwhelm them, jeopardizing learning in other areas (e.g. technique). Instead, try using a spirit of playfulness to motivate the children and to promote creative play and allow them to enjoy playing without worrying. At this age, children should be encouraged to learn how to search for and find successful action solutions (techniques) and game situation solutions (tactics) for themselves in free play. Although free play will become increasingly tactical in the course of the Futsal player's development, in the training and play of 6-8 year-olds, their typical urge to move and playfulness should not be sacrificed for the sake of tactical pressures (fear of failure, etc.).

Despite a few performance-limiting developmental milestones in 6-8 year-olds, the gross forms of the basic techniques of dribbling, passing and shooting at the goal can already be taught at this age. Although training itself is not systematic yet, there should be a systematic alternation between drills and play.

Because of the above-mentioned coordination problems and the children's low level of experience with the ball, they must first get used to how the ball rolls and bounces, and a variety of drills and games that focus on this should therefore be included in every training session. If possible, using balls of different sizes, as this diverse movement experience will also develop the children's ball skills. The development of coordination must be a key content of games and drills for children of this age. This is best done with simple games of catch or easily mastered ball games. After the drills phase, the children should be allowed sufficient time to practice shooting at the goal in small groups. The training session should end with a brief, motivating final discussion.

Specializations have no place in this age group!The development of all-round, basic motor skills, coordination, skill and creativity is much more important and can be achieved by means of playful drills, small-sided games or competitions, not only with a Futsal ball but with different types of ball, hand apparatus or even everyday objects.

The most important techniques to be taught in this age group are dribbling, passing with the inside of the shoe and shooting at the goal, so drills that combine these elements should therefore be performed. Variants of shooting at the goal allow children to learn the techniques in a playful way, and every session should conclude with shooting at the goal if possible.

The secret of ball control, and therefore of being a good player, is plenty of contact with the ball. This can be achieved by means of dribbling drills, the use of more than one ball, practicing in small groups or task setting that avoids children having passive roles. They promote ball control and allow the children to gain confidence with the ball.

The reduced bounce of the Futsal ball provides a huge advantage over the normal soccer ball; it is much easier for children to control. Even the technically weaker players are able to achieve good results more quickly.

Pure tactics have no place in training for this age group either. Tactical training is usually based on the performance of 'fun' drills that allow the children to get used to the 'tactical system' without necessarily being aware that they are doing so.

The coaching of tactics is therefore reduced to the teaching of a differentiated age-appropriate reaction to diverse match situations.

The tactical goals that should be met in this age group are:

- Learning of general and basic concepts, for example 'attacker', 'teammate', and 'opponent'.
- Using real match situations reduced to 1 v 1 or 2 v 2 etc. , in order to encourage the players' decision-making ability.
- Practicing simple tactical aspects resulting from techniques learnt in this age group.

Therefore:

- Learn through play.
- Learn simple tactical aspects via the different techniques.
- And, if possible, learn basic concepts like 'striker', 'defender', 'teammate' and 'opponent.

4.1.1   Basic technique drills

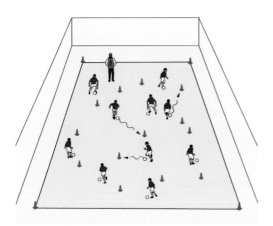

Skittle Futsal

Emphasis: Passing.

Equipment: 1 ball per child, 10-15 cones.

Set-up: Pitch approx. 22 x 22 yards, cones are distributed all over the pitch.

Implementation: Every child tries to knock over as many cones as possible by kicking the ball. After about 10 seconds, the coach starts to put the cones back in place.

Duration: Unspecified.

Alternative: Competition 'coach against players', can the players knock all the cones over?

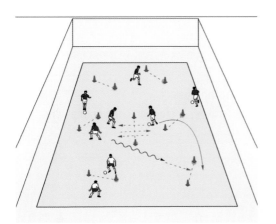

Passing through Cone Goals

Emphasis: Passing.

Equipment: At least 2 cones per pair, 1 ball per pair.

Set-up: Pitch approx. 22 x 22 yards, several 2-yard wide cone goals.

Implementation: The pairs pass the ball to each other three times through one cone goal then move on to the next one, and so on. Which team can pass through all the cone goals most quickly?

Duration: Unspecified.

Alternative: With obstructing player (coach).

Hoop Jumping

Emphasis: Dribbling.

Equipment: 1 ball per child, 10-15 hoops.

Set-up: Pitch approx. 22 x 22 yards, hoops spread out over the pitch.

Implementation: The players dribble through the hoop circuit, before the hoops they stop the ball with the sole of the foot and lob the ball over the hoop.

Variation: Hold the ball between the feet and jump over the hoop.

Duration: Unspecified.

Alternatives: Competitions

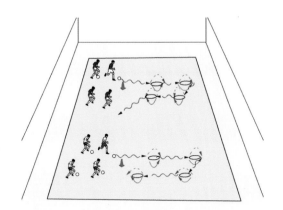

- Which player can lob the most hoops in 1 minute?
- Which player can jump over the most hoops in 1 minute?

Points of the Compass

Emphasis: Dribbling.

Equipment: 1 ball per player, 4 cones, if possible bibs.

Set-up: Mark out pitch approx. 22 x 22 yards with cones. The four sides are named for the points of the compass (north, south, east, west).

Implementation: The players move around with the ball on the pitch. When the coach calls out one of the points of the compass, the players dribble quickly to the appropriate line.

Duration: Unspecified.

Alternative: Team competition

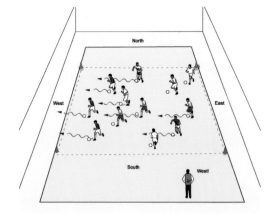

- Form several teams, the team of the player who is last to dribble to the line loses.

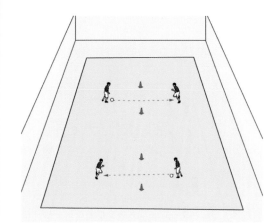

Cone Goal

Emphasis: Shooting at the goal.

Equipment: 1 ball per pair, several cones.

Set-up: Set up several 3.5-yard wide goals with the cones.

Implementation: Shoot with the instep through the cone goals from about 11 yards away. Practice with both feet! Who can score the most goals out of 10 attempts?

Duration: Unspecified.

Alternatives:

- Reduce the distance (easier).
- Increase the distance (harder).

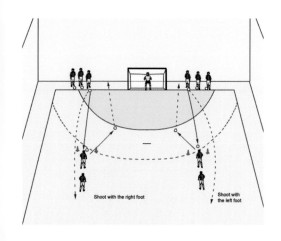

Shoot with the right foot

Shoot with the left foot

10 Shots at the Goal

Emphasis: Shooting at the goal.

Equipment: Several balls per team, 4 cones.

Set-up: 2 teams.

Implementation: The player on the goal line passes to the player in the cone goal, who traps the ball and runs with it forward and inward, and shoots at the goal. Every team has 10 shots. Which team scores the most goals? Then change sides (practice shooting with both feet).

Duration: Unspecified.

Alternative: Throw the ball to teammates who must catch it then volley it with the right and left feet.

Goal Scoring Contest 2 v 2

Emphasis: Shooting at the goal

Equipment: Approx. 10 balls, approx. 16 cones

Set-up: Several cones goals are set up across the sports hall, with a distance of approx. 13 yards between the goals, the goal shooting line is about 7 yards away. The group is split into teams of two.

Implementation: 2 teams play against each other, each team has 10 shots on goal, one person on each team is a goalkeeper, the other shoots from the shooting line (7 yards). Swap roles after 5 shots.

Duration: Unspecified.

Alternative: Shots at the goal after pass by partner – 'dog eat dog' competition. Who scores the most goals?

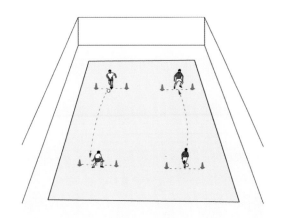

Juggling King

Emphasis: Coordination.

Equipment: 1 ball per child.

Set-up: Half a pitch.

Implementation: The players hold the ball in their hands. On a signal from the coach, each player juggles the ball with his foot (feet). The ball should not touch the ground. How many times do the children touch the ball in 1 minute? How many times do the children touch the ball in 3 x 1 minute (total contacts)?

Duration: Unspecified.

Alternative: Practice with various different balls.

Tip: Include as many training sessions as possible.

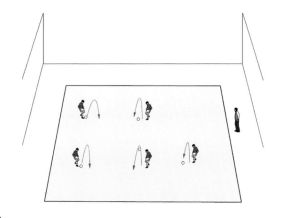

4.1.2 Small-sided games and training games

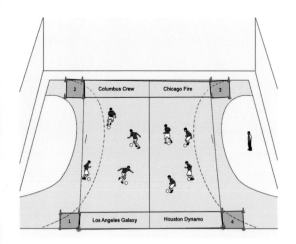

Major League

Emphasis: Small-sided game.

Equipment: 1 ball per player, 16 cones.

Set-up: Pitch 13 x 13 yards.

Implementation: Players dribble randomly, when the coach calls the name of a club, all the players dribble as fast as possible to that section. The last three players must complete a funny forfeit.

Duration: Unspecified.

Alternatives:

- Use numbers or colors instead of club names.
- Form several small teams.
- The team of the player who comes in last loses.
- You can also play for points. Which team has most points after 10 tries?
- A ranking list is also motivating.

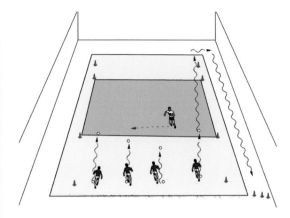

The Guardian of the Bridge

Emphasis: Dribbling.

Equipment: 1 ball per player, 8 cones.

Set-up: Pitch approx. 11 x 22 yards, including a 'bridge' of about 11 x 6 yards.

Implementation: The dribblers try to get past the 'guardian of the bridge' to the other side. The guardian tries to kick away as many balls as possible. The players who lose their ball on the 'bridge' become new guardians.

Duration: Unspecified.

Alternatives:

- Each player is a guardian 3 times. Who captures the most balls?
- 10 attempts, who is guardian the fewest times?

Gigantic Goals

Emphasis: Small-sided game.

Equipment: Balls, goal posts, cones, thick mats (if available).

Set-up: Depending on the size of the hall, mark out pitches of 2 x 16 x 13 yards or 2 x 11 x 13 yards.

Implementation: 3 v 3 or 4 v 4 (so that nobody is left out!). Free play into gigantic goals with no goalkeeper! The large goals enable many goals to be scored celebrated!

Duration: Unspecified.

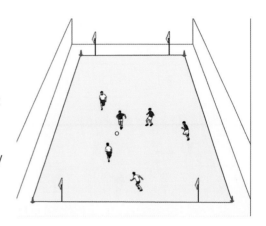

3 Goal Match

Emphasis: Small-sided game.

Equipment: 12 cones, at least 3 balls, different colored bibs.

Set-up: Play across the hall. On the sidelines mark approx. 16 x 12 yards pitch 3 goals one every 6 yards.

Implementation: Three groups: two players of each group play 1 v 1 simultaneously. The ball-carrying player may play to all three of the opponent's goals. The non ball-carrying players stop the balls behind the goals. After 30 seconds (up to a maximum of 1 minute), three different pairs play 1 v 1.

Duration: Unspecified.

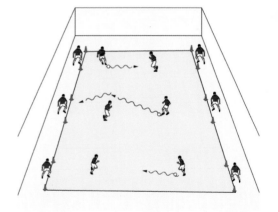

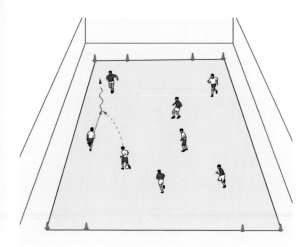

Dribbling Goals

Emphasis: Small-sided game.
Equipment: 8 cones, ball, bibs.
Set-up: Play across the hall. On the touchlines, a 19 x 25 yard pitch is marked with 2 dribbling goals at each end (about 9 yards).
Implementation: Play 4 v 4 (5 v 5), the aim of the game is to dribble into the opponent's dribbling goal (= goal!)
Duration: Unspecified.

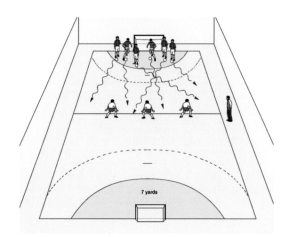

Dribbling King

Emphasis: Small-sided game.
Equipment: 1 ball per dribbling player.
Set-up: Whole pitch.
Implementation: On a signal from the coach, all dribbling players try to reach the other side of the sports hall.
3 defenders try to stop them between the 11-yard markings. The players whose balls are cleared away become the new defenders.
Duration: Unspecified.
Alternative: Each player acts as a defender 3 times. Who can steal the most balls?

Defending Party

Emphasis: Small-sided game.

Equipment: 1 ball and 6 cones per pitch.

Set-up: Mark out several 16 x 19 yard pitches. The cones are placed about 4 yards apart.

Implementation: Play 1 v 1 towards the cones. The player with the ball tries to hit one of his opponent's cones. If he succeeds, he takes it with him to his goal line. A player has lost when he only has 1 cone left.

Duration: Unspecified.

Alternatives:

- Set a time limit
- Count the cone goals
- Play matches
- Can also be played 2 v 1 or 2 v 2

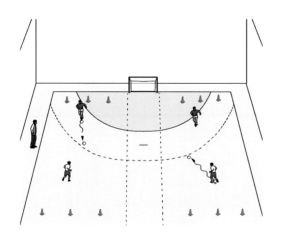

3 v 3 with 3 Goals

Emphasis: Small-sided game.

Equipment: 1 ball, 12 cones, bibs.

Set-up: Mark out with cones 3 small goals along each touchline of an approx. 21 x 16 yard pitch.

Implementation: Play 3 v 3 into 3 goals. The attacking team should attack all three of the opposing team's goals.

Duration: Approx. 3 minutes per game.

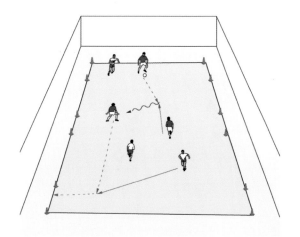

4.1.3 Basic tactical rules

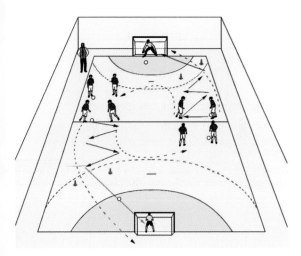

One-Two Passing

Emphasis: Basic tactical rules.

Equipment: 1 ball per pair, 4 cones.

Set-up: Whole hall, circuit.

Implementation: Two groups start at the same time from the center line. 2 players from one group play one-two passes to each other then shoot at the goal from a marked shooting line.

The players run to the other group and swap positions from outside to inside and vice versa to ensure that they practice with both feet.

Duration: Unspecified.

Alternative: Which pair scores the most goals?

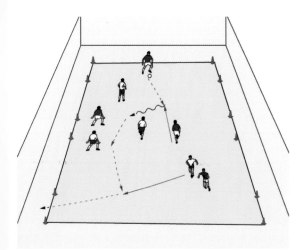

Left and Right Count Double

Emphasis: Basic tactical rules.

Equipment: 1 ball, 12 cones, bibs.

Set-up: Mark out with cones 3 small goals along each touchline of an approx. 26 x 16 yard pitch.

Implementation: Play 4 v 4 into 3 small goals. The attacking team may attack all 3 of the opposing team's goals. Goals scored in the outside goals (left and right) count double.

Duration: Approx. 4 minutes per game.

4.1.4 Conditioning drills

Bear Hunt

Emphasis: Conditioning.
Equipment: Cones.
Set-up: Pitch marked with a gap of at least 2 yards between the pitch and the wall of the sports hall.
Implementation: A hunter goes on a 'bear hunt' and tries to catch as many 'bears' as possible within a given time. The trapped 'bears' must sit down, but can be set free by other 'bears' who give them a 'high five'.
Duration: 30-60 seconds per run-through.
Alternative: Send more hunters on the bear hunt (2-3). Who can catch the most bears?

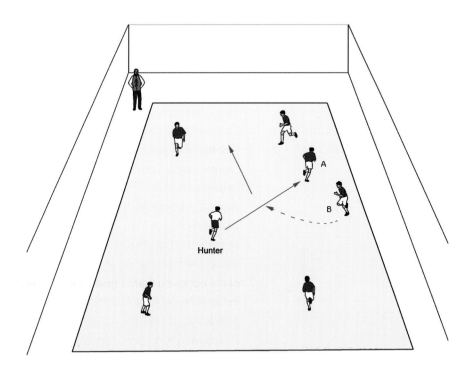

4.1.5 Coordination

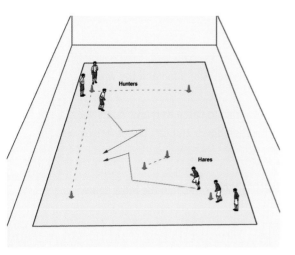

Hare and Hunter

Emphasis: Coordination.

Equipment: 5 cones per pitch.

Set-up: Mark out several approx. 11 x 11 yard pitches.

Implementation: The hare stands in a corner of the pitch, the hunter stands in the diagonally opposite corner, about 3 yards inside the pitch. As soon as the hare comes out of his form and runs past the cone goal, the hunter is off. The hare tries to run along one of the two lines without being caught by the hunter. Then swap roles and positions.

Duration: 30-60 seconds per run-through.

Alternative: The hare must run through the cone goal.

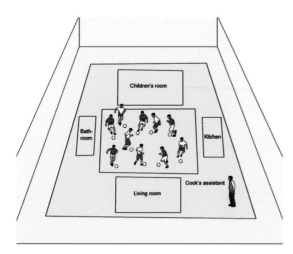

Tidying up the House

Emphasis: Coordination (with the ball)

Equipment: 1 ball per player, 20 cones.

Set-up: Mark out a 22 x 22 yard pitch; behind each sideline a room is marked out.

Implementation: The children move around the pitch performing different tasks (rolling the ball, dribbling the ball with the sole of the foot, etc.). On a command from the coach (e.g. 'children's room'), the ball must be placed in the corresponding room (not kicked!), after which the players return to the pitch.

Duration: Unspecified.

Alternative: The last three players must perform a funny forfeit. Form 2 teams. The team of the player who is last to return to the pitch has lost ('group punishment').

Shoot and Hurdle

Emphasis: Coordination.

Equipment: 1 ball per player, 4 cones, 2-4 hurdles.

Set-up: Circuit, with 2-4 hurdles placed along the route.

Implementation: The players kick the ball through the cone goals, run around them, collect the ball again and dribble up to shooting line (7 yard line), from where they shoot at the goal and then take the place of the keeper. The freed keeper collects the ball, kicks the ball under the first hurdle, runs around it and lobs (throws) the ball over the second hurdle.

Duration: Unspecified.

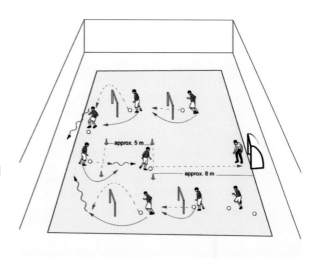

Circuit

Emphasis: Coordination.

Equipment: Balls, 8 cones, gymnastic poles, gymnastic hoops.

Set-up: Course covering either half of or the whole hall.

Implementation: Both groups start at the same time and pass the ball forward. The player in the first group skips over the gymnastic poles, gets behind his ball, dribbles through the cone goal and joins the other group. The player from the second group hops through the hoops, gets behind his ball then dribbles through the cone goal to join the other group.

Duration: Unspecified.

Alternative: Different types of jumping.

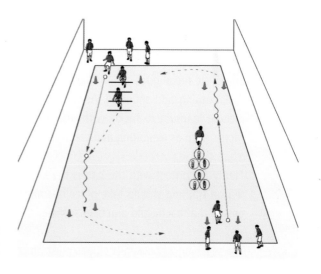

4.2   Training for 8-10 year-olds

The 8-10 year-old category that follows the 6-8 year play-phase is the ideal period for learning the basics. This golden age (which can last until the age of 12) offers ideal preconditions for great learning progress in technique training. While children's musculature is still quite undeveloped and coordination may still be problematic, this is just the right time for children to learn new things.

The training content is the same as in the younger age group:
Skill, running with the ball, passing, controlling the ball, dribbling, scoring, should all be presented in an age-appropriate way.

Some players may already have a good mastery of the basic, individual Futsal techniques in an overall form. However, there should be no specialization; a wide range of skills helps the all-round development of the young player's talents.

To achieve this, target-oriented tasks must be practiced with the ball in training. The inclusion of small-sided games in addition to Futsal promotes an all-around sporting experience. However, more space must now be given to the systematic learning and consolidation of the basic techniques.

The basic techniques are the technical skills of running with the ball, controlling the ball, passing and shooting. As well as these basic techniques, training contents also include learning to tackle with and around the ball and the beginnings of learning tactics such as exploiting and creating space and playing as a team.

Plenty of contact with the ball is the key to learning basic Futsal techniques. For this reason training should take place in small groups to avoid long waiting times and to ensure that each child practices sufficiently.

The teaching of basic techniques must always be done via age-appropriate, motivating and playful drills. Monotonous, boring tasks are counterproductive and take the fun out of the game for the young player. Drills should therefore not be presented as an unnecessary evil, small-sided games (with targeted technical elements) are highly demanding and the technique is learnt or improved almost without the players noticing.

In order to be able to teach the basic techniques in an age-appropriate and motivating way, the coach must not only possess an extensive repertoire of drills and game forms, he must above all consider the sport biological characteristics of the learning group concerned:

6-8 year-olds still have ongoing movement problems due to the height growth spurt. 8-10 year-olds are able to move more harmoniously due to the strong development of the musculature in this age group. This physical development leads to a significant improvement both in conditioning and coordination. This improvement continues until around age 12. This increase in physical strength and ability is accompanied by the development of the child's self-confidence and curiosity. The child seeks out physical activity and wants to measure himself against others.

The above-mentioned physical and psychological developmental milestones offer optimal preconditions for the fast and easy learning of the necessary technical skills, at least in their gross form.

Pure strength drills are not appropriate for this age group either, although endurance can be practiced slightly more. This can be done by means of fun catching, ball and relay games, which do not require long introductions. Children don't like to hang around. The use of a hurdle circuit also promotes movement skills. A special warm-up program is still not necessary, as children want and should get going quickly straight away and obey their urge to move.

The training forms are mainly determined by the above-described developmental milestones:

Futsal-specific coordination training with the ball, fun technique training with motivating contests and games and finally 'little Futsal games' with appropriate emphases in which the children can try out the techniques they have been practicing. It is important to let the players make mistakes and to praise what they have learnt.

The enjoyment of play and movement can be taken for granted here; competition and measuring oneself against others are highly motivating.

For children, ideal game forms provide the opportunity for plenty of contact with the ball, which can be ensured either by reducing the size of the pitch, reducing the size of the team or by a combination of both. These measures also necessarily allow weaker players to participate in games as it is less easy for them to avoid joining in.

Reducing the pitch size in particular requires the fast play typical of Futsal, although the more easily controlled Futsal ball helps both the beginner or weaker player as well as the advanced talent to achieve good results.

Futsal's sometimes complex rules must be adapted to the age group and simplified, but without losing the basic philosophy of Futsal.
In any case, every training session must allow enough room for free Futsal play, and additional tasks can be included for other emphases.

Variety in the game forms and multi-faceted movement tasks help to overcome the still poor concentration ability of this age group; the child who is challenged in an age-appropriate and varied way will be more likely to stay focused. This also develops self-confidence. The young athlete who is able to successfully complete the tasks set for him will be motivated for the long-term.

Make sure that the degree of difficulty is appropriate, as children will find overly simple drills boring and not feel a sense of satisfaction after completing the task.

Another objective during this age group is that of fostering team spirit. This can be done by means of team games in differing team sizes. The emphasis should therefore be placed on Futsal games with goals in small teams. The children must be able to experience goal-scoring as the result of a collaborative effort.

4.2.1 Basic technique drills

Gap Game

Emphasis: Passing.
Equipment: 1 ball and 2 cones per two players.
Set-up: Whole hall, practice in pairs.
Implementation: The players stand facing each other about 9 yards apart and pass the ball to each other through an approx. 2-yard-wide cone goal. Don't forget to practice with both feet!
Duration: Unspecified.
Alternatives:

* Widen the cone goals (easier) or narrow them (harder).
* Which pair can manage 10 passes without making a mistake?
* Which pair can pass to each other for the longest time without making a mistake?

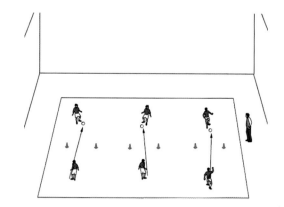

Wall Pass

Emphasis: Passing.
Equipment: 1 ball per player, approx. 8 benches, 12 cones.
Set-up: Whole hall, 3 pitches of equal size marked out with cones; 4 benches are placed at an angle in the two outside pitches.
Implementation: The children start by dribbling in the center pitch. When the coach points to an outside pitch, all the children must dribble toward this pitch and kick the ball 5 times against a bench.
Duration: Unspecified.
Alternative: After completing the task, dribble back to the center pitch and put your hand up holding the ball. Who can do it first?

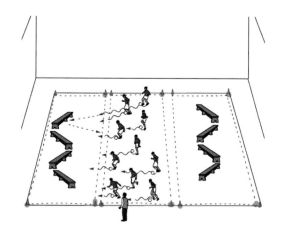

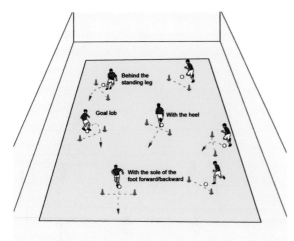

Goal of the Month

Emphasis: Dribbling.

Equipment: 1 ball per player, 1 goal formed from 2 cones per player.

Set-up: One dribbling pitch (approx. 22 x 22 yards) with several cone goals.

Implementation: The players dribble around the pitch and shoot at the goal following instructions of the 'goal of the month': with the heel, lobbing, behind the standing leg, with the toes, pull the ball forward, backward, forward with the sole of the foot and let the ball roll into the goal, etc.

Duration: Unspecified.

Alternative: Who can accomplish the set task quickest at five goals?

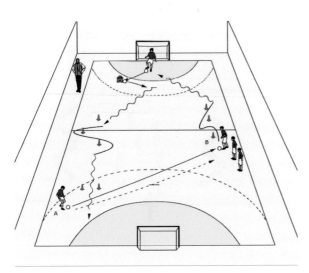

Circuit with Dribbling, Passing, Ball Receiving and Dampening

Emphasis: Complex drill for basic techniques.

Equipment: 1 ball per player, 10 cones, 1 long bench.

Set-up: Whole hall, set up the circuit as in the diagram.

Implementation: Player A passes to player B on the opposite side of the pitch and runs after his pass. Player B dribbles through the cone slalom and then passes to the keeper, who catches the ball and throws it back to player B, who traps it and runs with it. He then kicks the ball against a bench, controls the ball again and dribbles through the second cone slalom. After the last cone he sprints through a cone goal about 11 yards away. He then runs to stand in line.

Duration: Unspecified.

Pitch Change

Emphasis: Playful dribbling drill.

Equipment:1 ball per child, 12 cones, bibs.

Set-up: 2 dribbling pitches (approx. 11 x 11 yards) marked out about 11 yards apart. About 11 yards apart along the center line mark out 2 x 3 yard-wide cone goals. 1 team per pitch.

Implementation: The children dribble in their team's pitch and follow the coach's instructions (with the weak foot, with the

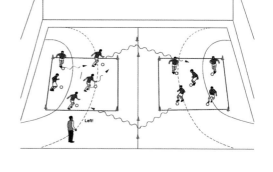

sole of the foot, etc.). On the command 'left' or 'right', the teams change pitches by running through the cone goal on the left or right of their running direction.

Duration: Unspecified.

Alternatives:

*   The players react to a visual signal (e.g. 'red bib' = round to the left, 'yellow bib' = round to the right).
*   Dribble around a complete circuit.
*   Competition: which team gets all its members into the new pitch first? The winning team gets 2 points. Which team is first to 10 points?

Goalkeeper

Emphasis: Goal shooting technique drill.

Equipment: 6 cones per pitch, 4 poles per pitch, several balls per pitch.

Set-up: Mark out several 17 x 11 yard pitches crossways across the hall.

Implementation: Position 3 players between 2 posts. A starts, dribbles briefly then shoots at B's goal. B then dribbles and shoots at C's goal, etc. Have several balls ready at each goal.

Duration: Unspecified.

Alternative:

*   Widen (easier) or narrow (harder) the goals.
*   Competition: who is the first to score 10 goals? The winners then play off against each other.

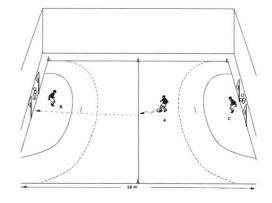

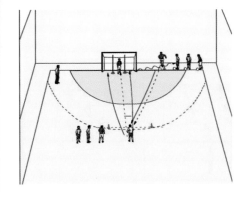

Left and Right Count

Emphasis: Goal shooting technique drill.

Equipment: 2 goals, 4 posts, 8 cones, several balls per goal.

Set-up: Whole hall, practice down both sides in parallel.

Implementation: One child stands without a ball at the shooting line, one acts as ball retriever in the goal between the posts, the other with the ball at the starting cone. The child at the starting cone passes the ball with an instep kick through the cone goal. The child there stops the ball behind the line and shoots with an instep kick into goal. Only kicks into the outside corners of the goal count. The ball retriever in the goal takes the ball and goes to stand in line, the passer goes to replace him in goal and the goalkeeper becomes the ball retriever in the goal.

Duration: Unspecified.

Alternatives:

- Competition: Goal A against goal B, which team is first to score 10 goals?
- Only pass with the weaker foot.
- Only shoot at the goal with the weaker foot.

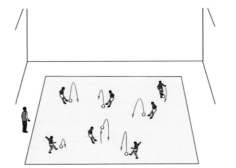

Dampening the Ball

Emphasis: Dribbling and coordination.

Equipment: 1 ball per pair.

Set-up: Either half the hall or the whole hall depending on the number of players.

Implementation: Player A throws the ball up in the air to player B, who dampens the ball, controls it and dribbles about 3-4 yards. He then picks up the ball and throws it up in the air back to player A.

Duration: Unspecified.

Alternatives:

- Do the drill on the run.
- Practice with the left and right feet.

4.2.2 Small-sided games and training games

Major League I

Emphasis: Small-sided game.
Equipment: 8 balls, depending on available facilities (see below) cones, benches, boxes, posts.
Set-up: Play across the hall. Mark out 8 pitches using the floor markings or cones. Mark out goals using boxes, cones or posts.
Implementation: Play 1 v 1 simultaneously on all 8 pitches. The winner of a game gets 3 points, in the case of a draw, each player gets 1 point. After each game, one player from each pitch moves clockwise to the next pitch.
Duration: Approx. 30 seconds per game.
Alternatives:
* Each player plays for his favorite team.
* Add up points and set up league tables.

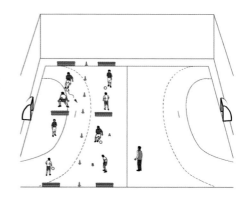

Major League II

Emphasis: Small-sided game.
Equipment: Depending on the facilities available (see below), 4 balls, bibs.
Set-up: Whole hall, mark out 4 pitches using the floor markings or cones. Mark out goals with benches, boxes, cones or posts.
Implementation: Play 2 v 1 on all pitches simultaneously, swapping over. The larger team tries to score a goal against its lone opponent. If they succeed, or if the defender scores a goal, the larger and smaller teams swap over. All the teams play against each other.
Duration: Until a goal is scored, but not more than 1 minute.
Alternative: Which team scores the most goals?
* Each team chooses the name of a club, set up a league table.

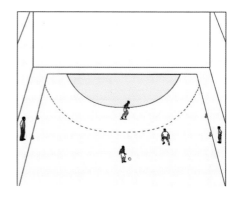

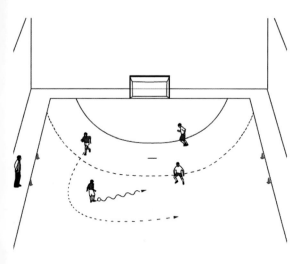

Major League III

Emphasis: Small-sided game.

Equipment: Depending on available facilities (see below), 4 balls, bibs.

Set-up: Whole hall, mark out 4 pitches using the floor markings or cones. Mark out goals with boxes, cones or posts.

Implementation: On all 4 pitches play 2 v 2 simultaneously, swapping over. Give the teams names of Major League clubs and set up a league table. After every game, on all 4 pitches change always the same teams in a clockwise direction. Every pitch is given a stadium name, e.g. Rose Bowl, Cotton Bowl, Giants Stadium, etc.

Duration: About 30-60 seconds per game. Monitor the intensity!

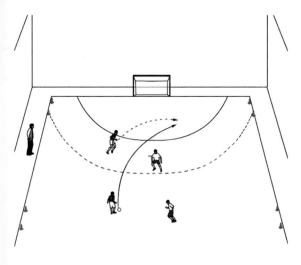

2 v 2 into 4 Goals

Emphasis: Small-sided game.

Equipment: 2 balls, 16 cones, bibs.

Set-up: Play across the hall. In each half, 4 goals are marked out with cones along the sidelines with a width of 2-3 yards depending on the players' ability.

Implementation: Play 2 v 2 into 4 goals, all teams play each other. The winner gets 3 points, in the case of a draw, both teams get 1 point. Add the points and set up a league table.

Duration: Not longer than 2 minutes per game.

Alternative: Who is the four-goal champion?

3 v 3 without Goalkeeper

Emphasis: Small-sided game.
Equipment: 1 ball, bibs, 2 goals
(possibly mats). Posts or cones (depending
on equipment available).
Set-up: Mark out a 22 x 16 yard pitch. On
both touchlines, set up 1 (mat) goal and
2 post goals for each team.
Implementation: The teams play 3 v 3 in
free play to all the opposing teams' goals.
Duration: Unspecified.
Alternative: Play 4 v 4 with goalkeeper. If
there are several teams, play a tournament.

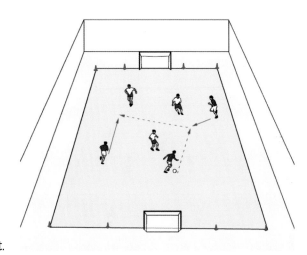

4 v 4 with One Goal

Emphasis: Small-sided game.
Equipment: 1 ball, 4 cones, 1 goal, bibs.
Set-up: Mark out a 22 x 26 yard pitch and
a boundary line.
Implementation: Team A starts with 4
players and 1 goalkeeper, team B with 4
players on the pitch. Team A defends the
goal with the goalkeeper and starts a
counterattack after gaining possession of
the ball. They try to dribble over team B's
boundary line.
Duration: Unspecified.
Alternative: Play for time of change after
5 boundary line goals.

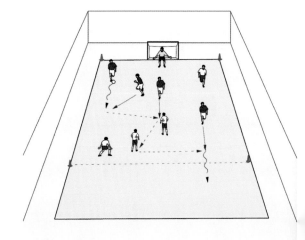

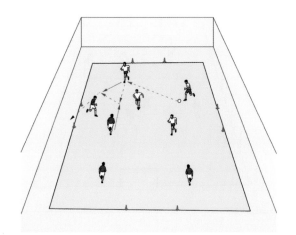

4 v 4 into Small Goals

Emphasis: Small-sided game.
Equipment: 1 ball, 12 cones, bibs.
Set-up: Mark out a 22 x 27 yard pitch. On each boundary line set up a 2.5-3.5 yard wide cone goal.
Implementation: Play 4 v 4 into 4 small goals. Each team defends 2 diagonally opposite goals and attacks the other two.
Duration: About 4 minutes.

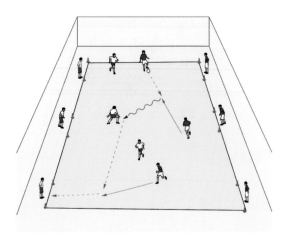

3 v 3 into 3 Small Goals

Emphasis: Small-sided game.
Equipment: 1 ball, 12 cones, bibs.
Set-up: Mark out a 16 x 22 yard pitch. Along each touchline mark out with cones 3 small 2. 5 yard wide goals.
Implementation: The teams play 3 v 3 into 3 small goals in alternation. A total of 12 players are divided into 2 groups of 6 players. Three players from each group play 3 v 3; the other 3 players wait behind a goal.
Duration: 2 minutes, then swap over.
Alternative: The team that scores a goal stays on the pitch, the other swaps with the team waiting on its side.

4.2.3 Basic tactical rules

Take Positions

Emphasis: Basic tactical rules.

Equipment: 1 ball, 2 goals (or mats), bibs.

Set-up: Mark out a pitch measuring 16 x 22 yards or 22 x 28 yards depending on the number of players.

Implementation: Depending on the number of children, form teams of 3 or 4 (defender, midfield, forward). Each team plays against all the other teams.

Duration: Unspecified.

Alternative: With or without goalkeeper (more chances of scoring a goal).

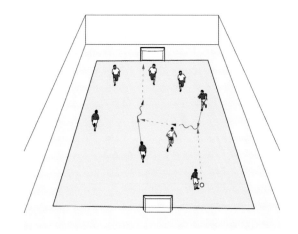

1 v 1 to 4 v 4

Emphasis: Basic tactical rules.

Equipment: 1 ball, 4 cones, bibs.

Set-up: Mark out a pitch according to the number of players: 1 v 1 about 11 x 16 yards, 4 v 4 about 16 x 22 yards.

Implementation: 1 v 1 to 4 v 4 play to 2 target lines. Free play, the team in possession of the ball should dribble over the opposing team's rear boundary line.

Duration: Unspecified.

Alternative: 2 neutral players are positioned on the sidelines making one team bigger than the other.

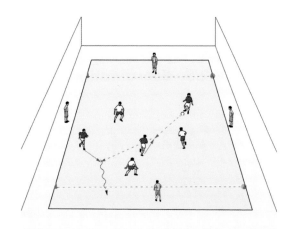

4.2.4 Conditioning drills

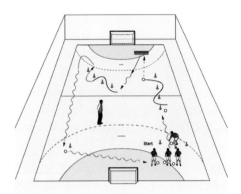

Cone Circuit

Emphasis: Conditioning.

Equipment: 1 ball per player, 12 cones, 1 long bench.

Set-up: The slalom course is marked out with cones covering the whole hall, the start and finish lines are marked with 3 cones.

Implementation: All players start at the starting line. As soon as the first player has passed the first cone, the next player starts. Dribble through the first cone slalom, kick against the bench, ball control and dribble through the second cone slalom, sprint with the ball to the next cone, collect the ball and juggle into the goal.

Duration: Unspecified.

Alternative: A certain number of timed run-throughs.

4.2.5 Coordination

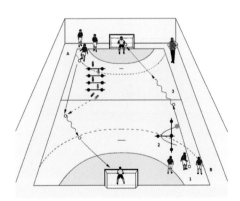

Dribbling Contest

Emphasis: Conditioning.

Equipment: 1 ball per player, about 7 gymnastic poles.

Set-up: Whole hall, circuit.

Implementation: 1 player each from groups A and B start at the same time. They kick their ball along the sideline, skip over the bars, control their ball again near the centerline, dribble briefly and shoot from the shooting line into the goal. They then line up with the ball in the other group.

Duration: Unspecified.

Alternative: 10 circuits, who scores the most goals?

Partner Kick
Emphasis: Coordination (with ball).
Equipment: Several balls, 10 cones, 2 goals.
Set-up: Use both goals and the whole hall. 7 yards in front of each goal a rectangle is marked out and another 3 yards in front a starting cone is placed. Two players wait beside the goal posts.

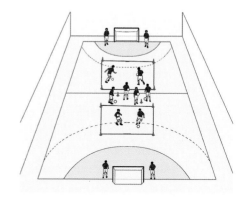

Implementation: On a signal from the coach, the first pair runs from the starting cone into their rectangle holding the ball. One throws, the other passes the ball flat to their partner. The player who catches the thrown ball then kicks it towards the goal while their partner kicks their ball from the floor. The players waiting at the goal retrieve the balls and then go to stand at the starting cones, while the strikers run to the goal, and so on.
Duration: Unspecified.
Alternative: A predetermined number of runthroughs.

Through the Rectangle to the Goal
Emphasis: Coordination (with ball).
Equipment: Several balls, 8 cones, 2 goals.
Set-up: Use the whole hall and two goals. 7 yards in front of the goal, mark out two rectangles and another 3 yards in front of it place 1 starting cone. 2 players wait near the goal posts.

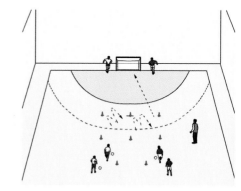

Implementation: On a signal from the coach, the first player runs from the starting cone with the ball in their hand to the rectangle, there kick the ball up twice with their thigh, catch it again and shoot at the goal. The players beside the goal posts retrieve the balls and go to stand at the starting cone. The strikers run to the goal.
Duration: Unspecified.
Alternative: Whose ball lands (first) in the net?

Slalom Variations

Emphasis: Coordination (with ball).

Equipment: Several balls, 8-12 poles.

Set-up: Half of the hall, 1 goal. 7-11 yards in front of the goal lay out two slalom courses.

Implementation: On a signal from the coach, the first players of each of the two groups start off and run through the slalom course (4-6 poles) and then shoot at the goal. Many variations are possible: backward, forward-backward, turning, uneven gaps between the poles, circling the pole, etc.

Duration: Unspecified.

Alternative: Which player scores first?

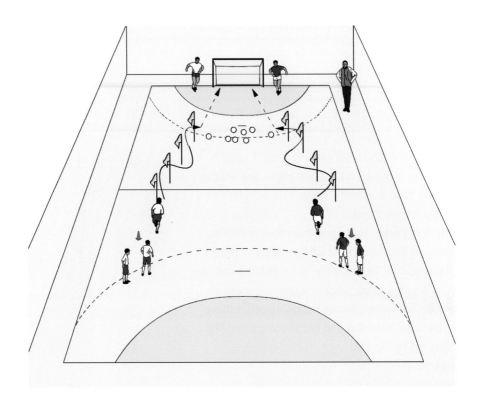

4.3   Training for 10-12 year-olds

The transition to the 10-12 age group represents a challenge for every coach, as adolescence is a difficult phase even for those going through it. Physical strength increases along with ability and motivation thus increasing the youngsters' self-confidence also. They start the gradual process of detachment from their parents and the coach also ceases to be the center of their world. Little by little, their peers take the place of adults. The respect and recognition of their teammates determines the role of the youngsters within the group.

Now that the players have mastered the different technical skills in their gross form in the preceding age groups, they must now refine and learn to also use them successfully when tackling an opponent for the ball. If they manage this, their team will treat them with great respect. Good prerequisites for this are tricks and feints that can never be better and more easily learnt than in this golden learning phase! In plentiful small-sided games with goals, the players must try out what they have learnt, make their own decisions and influence the match as they wish. These small-sided games with few players place great conditioning demands on the youngsters, making rest breaks essential. In these breaks the players can perform simple technical tasks which add variety to the small-sided games training format.

4.3.1 Basic technique drills

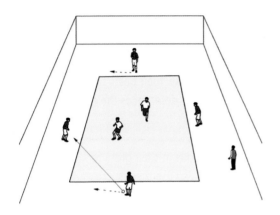

Role Swap

Emphasis: Passing.

Equipment: 1 ball, 4 cones, bibs if possible.

Set-up: Mark out a playing surface of about 11 x 16 yards.

Implementation: 2 defenders play against 4 forwards who move outside the pitch along the 'lines'. After a maximum of 3 ball contacts, the forwards must pass the ball safely and accurately across the pitch. If a defender takes the ball, the forward who loses the ball swaps roles with the defender who has been in the center of the pitch the longest.

Duration: Unspecified.

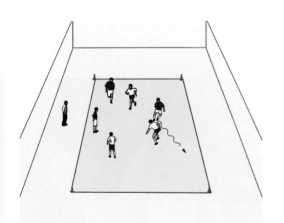

Dribbling Over the Touchline

Emphasis: Dribbling.

Equipment: 1 ball, 4 cones, bibs if possible.

Set-up: Mark out a pitch measuring about 16 x 22 yards, two teams of 3 players each.

Implementation: Play 3 v 3 with the aim of dribbling over the opposing team's touchline (= goal).

Duration: Unspecified.

Alternative: Change the teams more often. Simple ball drills can be performed in the breaks.

Shot at the GoalAfter One-Two

Emphasis: Shooting at the goal.

Equipment: 1 ball per player, 5 cones.

Set-up: Half the hall.

Implementation: Player A passes with the instep to player B and runs after his pass. Player B controls the ball and passes to player C. Player C plays a one-two with player B. Player B shoots at the goal with his instep, retrieves the ball and go back to stand in line.

Duration: The timing or the number of shots on goal per player can be determined in advance.

Alternative:

The drill can be set up in both halves of the hall, in which case the players must run first to the right then to the left (shoot with the left foot, shoot with the right foot). Who can score the most goals?

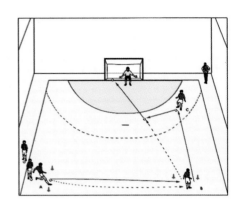

Juggling Champion

Emphasis: Coordination.

Equipment: 1 ball per player, 10 cones.

Set-up: Half the hall.

Implementation: The players stand at the start line holding the ball. Every player tries, while juggling the ball on their feet, to cross the first line without the ball touching the ground ('district champion'). Then they do the same again and try to reach the second line and become regional champion and so on until they become 'national champion'.

Duration: Unspecified.

Alternative: Practice with different balls (balloon, foam ball, etc.). Include similar forms of this drill in as many training sessions as possible.

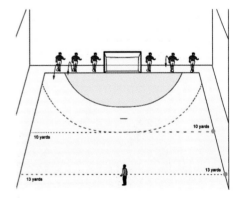

4.3.2 Small-sided games and training games

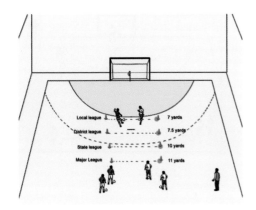

Promotion and Relegation

Emphasis: Goal-scoring.

Equipment: 3 balls per group of three, 8 cones, 1 goal, 1 post with foot.

Set-up: Half pitch, mark out four lines with cones according to the illustration. Divide the goal in two with the post. Divide the group into threes.

Implementation: The first player in each group of three tries to score from the 1st line into his half of the goal. If the second player in each group also scores from this line, his group is promoted. The group is relegated again if its players miss twice.

Duration: Unspecified.

Alternatives:

- Which group is first to reach the 'Major League' line?
- Place a neutral goalkeeper in goal instead of the post.

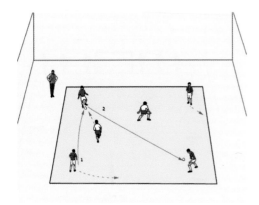

Passing and Worrying

Emphasis: Dribbling and passing.

Equipment: 1 ball per pitch, 8 cones, bibs.

Set-up: 2 pitches are marked out with cones. The players are divided into 3 teams of 2.

Implementation: Play 4 v 2. The four players try to get as much ball contact as possible by running cleverly. The 2 players in the center try to stop them. If they succeed, the pair whose pass was blocked must go into the center.

Duration: Unspecified.

Alternatives:

- Which pair manages to get most ball contact?
- Make the pitch smaller (easier) or bigger (harder).
- Limit ball contact.

Three Strikers against Two Defenders

Emphasis: Dribbling.

Equipment: 1 ball per pitch, 8 cones, bibs.

Set-up: Mark out two pitches with cones.

Implementation: Play 3 v 2 across goal lines. 3 players with the ball try to dribble over a goal line. Two defenders try to stop them and aim to score a goal with the ball if they win it. Defenders change after a certain time or after a certain number of goals.

Duration: Unspecified.

Alternative: 2 v 2 with one neutral player who always plays with the team in possession of the ball.

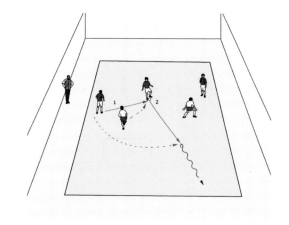

Burying the Balls

Emphasis: Passing and scoring.

Equipment: 10 balls, 4 cones, 2 goals, bibs.

Set-up: Mark out a pitch and 2 goals with cones. Divide the players into two teams.

Implementation: The coach stands with (10) balls outside the pitch and passes the first ball 'neutrally' into the pitch. Both teams should score as fast as possible into one of the goals. The coach then passes the next ball into the pitch.

Duration: Unspecified.

Alternative: Which team can 'bury' the most balls?

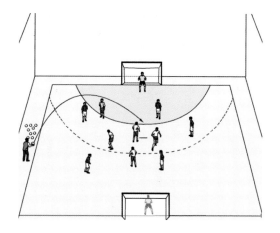

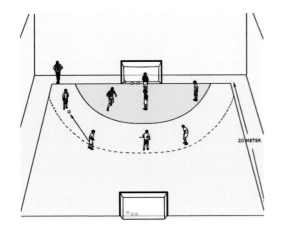

Overlap Attack

Emphasis: Passing and scoring.
Equipment: 1 ball, 4 cones, 2 goals, bibs.
Set-up: Mark out a 22 yard x 22 yard pitch and 2 goals with cones. Form 2 teams of 3 players and 2 neutral players.
Implementation: Play 3 v 2 neutral players against 2 + keeper. One player from the defending team goes into goal and his partner acts as a defender in front of the goal. The attackers, together with the neutral players, try to score. If they lose the ball or score a goal, the other team joins forces with the neutral players to form the outnumbering team.
Duration: Unspecified.

Attack Swap

Emphasis: Passing, dribbling, scoring.
Equipment: 2 balls, 16 cones, bibs.
Set-up: 1 pitch per half of the hall. Mark out 4 small goals (2.2 –3.3 yards) with 8 cones along the touchlines. Form four teams of three.
Implementation: Play 3 v 2, continuously changing the teams. 3 attackers try to score a goal against 2 defenders. If the 2 defenders win the ball, they pass back to their partner on the base line and now attack in turn as a team of three.
Duration: Unspecified.
Alternative: Play to a time limit or 10 attempts per team.

Blocking Shots on Goal I

Emphasis: Passing and shooting at the goal.
Equipment: 1 ball, 6 cones, bibs, 2 goals.
Set-up: Mark out a pitch with a centerline with 6 cones and 2 goals and divide the group into two teams.
Implementation: Play 4 v 2 plus 2 goalkeepers. The team with 2 players is placed in one half of the pitch and the team with 4 players in the other half. The players in the team of four pass the ball to each other, ready to shoot at the opposing team's goal when the timing is right. The opposing team tries to block possible passing paths and shots on goal.
Duration: Unspecified.
Alternative: Vary the distance from goal to goal depending on the players' ability. Continuously change the composition of the teams! Which team of 4 can score the most goals in 5 minutes?

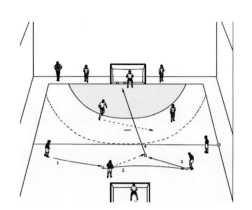

Blocking Shots on Goal II

Emphasis: Passing and shooting at the goal.
Equipment: 1 ball, 6 cones, 2 goals, bibs.
Set-up: A pitch is marked out with a center line with 6 cones and 2 goals, the players are divided into appropriate teams.
Implementation: Play 4 v 4 plus 2 goalkeepers. 2 teams of 4 players each move in their own halves. The players pass the ball among themselves waiting for the right moment to shoot at the opposing team's goal. The opposing team tries to block possible passing paths in their own half. After a shot at the goal, the other team may attack.
Duration: Unspecified.
Alternative: Vary the distance from goal to goal depending on the players' ability.

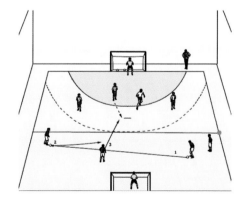

4.3.3 Basic tactical rules

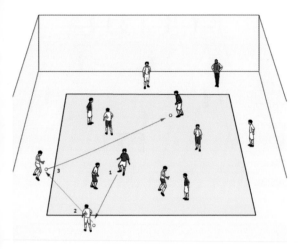

Emphasis: Passing.

Equipment: 1 ball, 4 cones, bibs.

Set-up: A 16 x 16 yard pitch is marked out with cones. The players are divided into appropriate teams.

Implementation: Play 4 v 4 plus 4. A group of 'neutral' players stands outside the pitch and plays with the team in possession of the ball. The first team to touch the ball ten times in a row moves to the outside.

Duration: Unspecified.

Alternatives:

- Limit the ball touches for the neutral players.
- Don't pass back to the same player.

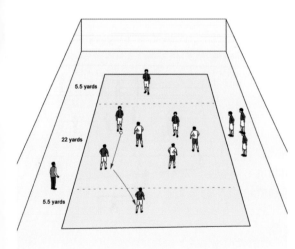

Zone Pass

Emphasis: Passing.

Equipment: 1 ball, 8 cones, bibs.

Set-up: Mark out a 22 x 22 yard pitch with cones and add two outside zones of 6 x 22 yards. Divide the players into appropriate teams.

Implementation: Play 5 v 3 from zone to zone. The team in possession of the ball joins forces with the neutral players outside the pitch, who may not be attacked, from outer zone to outer zone.

Duration: After 60 seconds, one team swaps with the players outside the pitch.

Alternative: Limit the number of times the players in the outer zones can touch the ball.

Joker

Emphasis: Passing.

Equipment: 1 ball, bibs.

Set-up: Whole pitch. Divide players into appropriate teams.

Implementation: Play 5 v 5 plus 1: a neutral player plays as joker with the team in possession of the ball. A team of 6 is always playing a team of 5, which is continuously changing.

Duration: Unspecified.

Alternative: Limit ball contact for the larger team and/or for the joker.

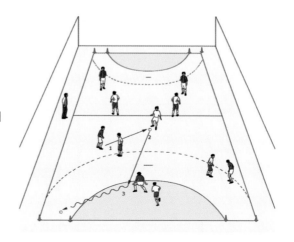

Quick Switch

Emphasis: Dribbling and shooting at the goal.

Equipment: 1 ball, 1 goal, 4 cones, bibs.

Set-up: In one half of the hall, mark out pitch with 1 goal and 2 small cone goals. Divide the players into 2 teams.

Implementation: Play 4 v 4 + goalkeeper into 2 'countergoals'. 4 players play to one goal with keeper. When they win the ball, the opposing team must try to score a goal as fast as possible in one of the small cone goals.

Duration: Unspecified.

Alternatives:

- Play to a time limit.
- Swap roles after 5 countergoals.
- Limit ball contact.
- Play via the goalkeeper.

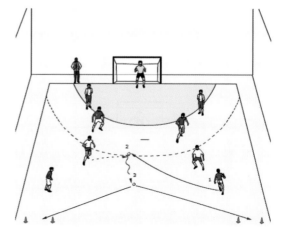

4.3.4 Conditioning drills

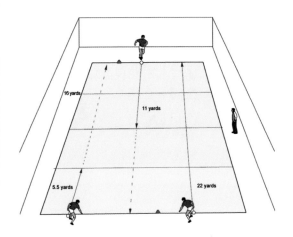

Line Running with Ball

Emphasis: Conditioning.

Equipment: Balls, cones.

Set-up: Whole pitch, marked out according to diagram.

Implementation: 2 players start at the same time with the ball on the starting line and run down the lines for 6-11 yards alternating between running fast and slowly.

Duration: 4 rounds in 4 minutes, with 2 minute rest breaks.

Alternative: Adjust the training load to players' ability, e.g. 4 rounds in 2 minutes, 2 minutes rest. It's not a competition! Individualize training!

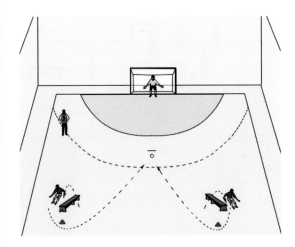

Sprint and Shoot

Emphasis: Conditioning.

Equipment: Balls, 1 goal, 2 benches, 2 cones.

Set-up: Use half a pitch.

Implementation: On a signal from the coach, the first players of both groups jump over the bench, sprint around the cones and then sprint to the ball. The faster player shoots at the goal, the other player retrieves the ball. Both players go back and stand in line.

Duration: Unspecified.

Alternatives:

- The groups swap positions (shoot with both left and right feet).
- Team competition: which group scores the most goals?
- Vary the number of jumps (between 1 and 10).

Conditioning Circuit

Emphasis: Conditioning.

Equipment: Balls, 2 long benches, 12 cones.

Set-up: Set up a circuit using the whole gym.

Implementation: The first player of both groups start from the starting line simultaneously. The players pass their ball forward, jump over the bench, control their balls before dribbling, dribble through the cone slalom and the shoot at the goal from a distance of about 11 yards. Then perform the drill from the other side.

Duration: Unspecified.

Alternatives:

- Two-legged jumping, hopping.
- Perform the drill to a time limit.
- Complete a certain number of circuits.

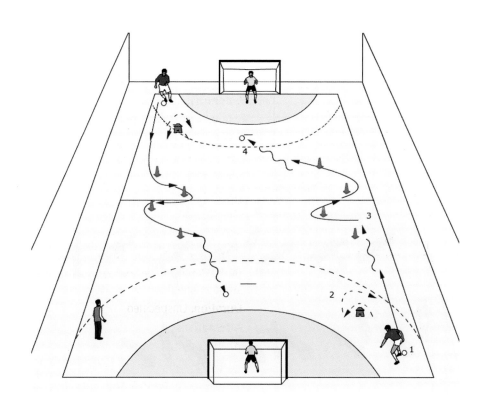

4.3.5 Coordination

Long Bench Circuit
Emphasis: Coordination.
Equipment: Balls, 6 benches or more (depending on available facilities).
Set-up: Use the whole hall. Place the benches parallel to each other about 2 yards apart.
Implementation: Slalom run forward, sideways and backward while bouncing the ball, slalom run and bounce off a bench, hopping slalom run with bounce, two-legged jumping on and off the benches with bounce, etc.
Duration: Unspecified.

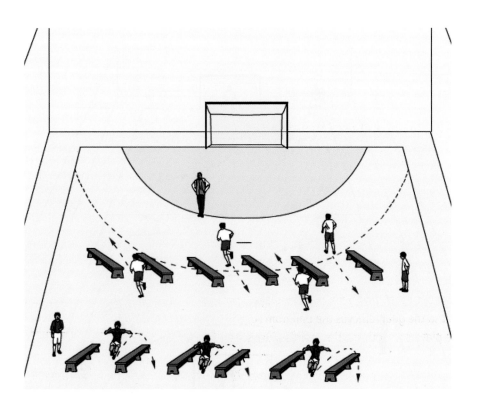

Circuit and Shoot

Emphasis: Coordination, shot at the goal.
Equipment: Balls, 2 goals, 2 mats, 8 cones.
Set-up: Use the whole hall.
Implementation: The first players in each group start simultaneously. They pass their ball forward, perform a forward roll, control the ball, dribble through the cone slalom and shoot at the goal from about 11 yards away (shooting line).
Duration: Unspecified.
Alternatives:

- Perform the circuit to a time limit.
- Complete a certain number of circuits.

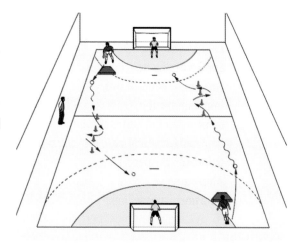

Circuit with Ball

Emphasis: Coordination, skill.
Equipment: Balls, 2 goals, cones.
Set-up: Whole hall, circuit with shot at the goal.
Implementation: Player A starts at a mark on the floor and dribbles through a cone slalom (1). From a marked rectangle about 4.5-9 yards in front of the goal depending on ability, A shoots at the goal (2).
At the same time, B starts in the opposite direction, passes the ball through a cone goal (4), runs in an arc outside past this (5), picks up the ball again and dribbles to the other circuit starting point (6). The player next to the goal retrieves the ball from A.

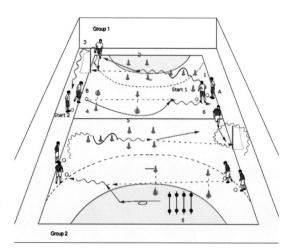

The players at both starting points always start simultaneously!
Duration: Unspecified.
Alternative: Put various different movement tasks on the running path: forward roll, jump over bib, balancing, juggling with the thigh, head, etc...

Pair Tag

Emphasis: Coordination.

Equipment: 8 cones.

Set-up: Half a hall, mark out a pitch leaving a gap of 1-2 yards between pitch and wall, form teams of two.

Implementation: On a signal from the coach, one pair tries to catch another pair. All pairs must hold hands throughout. The caught tandem must perform 5 push-ups and then catch another pair, etc.

Duration: Unspecified.

Alternatives:

- Play to a time limit: who can catch the most pairs in 1 minute?
- A caught pair must perform coordination exercises (e.g. forward roll).

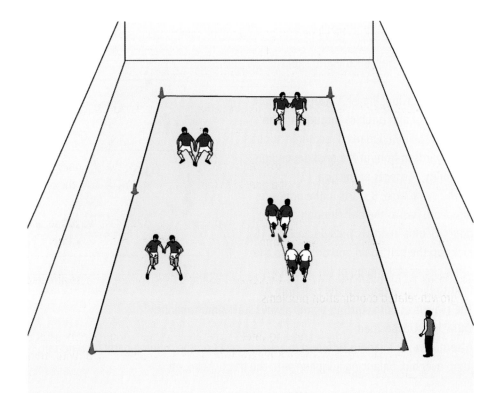

4.4   Training for 12-14 year-olds

By now, the players will have learnt technical, coordinative and early tactical skills in basic training.

The golden age of learning that was so successful for the players now ends due to a rapid growth spurt phase. For many adolescents, this growth spurt results in uncoordinated movements and temporary coordination problems. That is why the basic training of technical skills should end at the start of this critical phase.

The introduction of new techniques is not advisable as learning is slow in this age group. Focus instead on consolidating the techniques already learnt. In view of the psychological developmental state, the competitive nature of game forms provides an optimal refining and stabilizing learning effect. However, pure drill forms should also be included, and finally the significant differences in growth between individual players must be taken into account when planning the training content.

For example, players in the same age group may be more than a year apart in terms of their physical and psychological development. A height difference of 10-12 inches between players on the same team is by no means uncommon.

The skills acquired in the drills should also be able to be successfully deployed in a game form.

Because of the great diversity in this age group, the coach's role is particularly important. He must be an expert on the one hand and a friend and 'buddy' on the other.

He should choose a varied training structure and the choice of drill should refine and consolidate the techniques already learnt.

The focus should increasingly be on tactics and conditioning, as they are less affected by growth-related coordination problems.

This age is characterized by increasing intellectual development. The memory attains its highest level of receptivity, which means that players are able to deal with more difficult tactical content.

Youngsters should naturally not be overtaxed, which is why in this age group the focus is on the development of individual and group tactics. But also running into free space, using the whole pitch and understanding the game are things that a player with temporarily reduced technical ability can still manage successfully. Also the willingness to run – and therefore conditioning – becomes more and more important for a successful game. Futsal is all about performing as dynamically and fast as possible, for which muscle speed strength is paramount. This must therefore be trained and developed in a way that resembles how it is solicited in an actual match. Match-specific circuit training, for example, is very motivating for this age group and a welcome change from working in isolation on speed or mobility.

4.4.1 Basic technique drills

One-Two

Emphasis: Passing, shooting.

Equipment: Balls, 6 cones.

Set-up: Use the whole pitch.

Implementation: Two players play one-twos with the inside of the shoe down one half of the pitch. After the center line, the ball-carrying player dribbles toward the goal and shoots at the goal from a shooting line. He then swaps to join the other group.

Duration: Unspecified.

Alternatives:

- Timed runs
- Perform a certain number of runs
- Pass with the outside of the shoe.

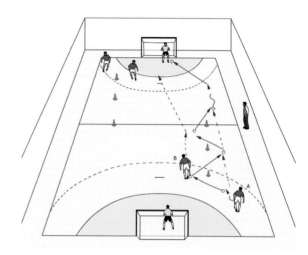

Ball Control I

Emphasis: Passing.

Equipment: Balls, cones.

Set-up: Whole hall, mark out two 11 x 11 yard squares.

Implementation: One player stands in each corner. A lobs the ball to B (C-D). B controls the ball with his thigh and then passes back to A (D-C).

Duration: Unspecified.

Alternative: Which team can play 10 passes without making a mistake? (The ball must land in the small square).

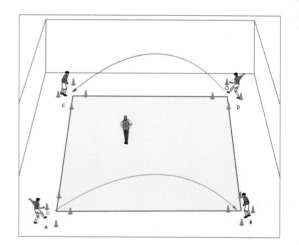

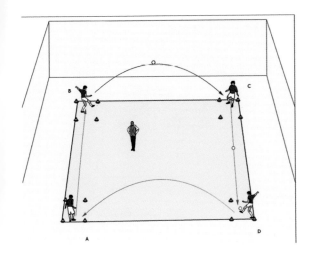

Ball Control II

Emphasis: Passing.

Equipment: Balls, cones.

Set-up: Mark out two 11 x 11 yard squares.

Implementation: One player stands in each corner.

A passes the ball to B – ball control!
B lobs the ball to C – ball control!
C passes the ball to D – ball control!
D lobs the ball to A – ball control!

Duration: Unspecified.

Alternatives:

- Play to a time limit
- A certain number of rounds.
- Which team can complete 5 rounds without making a mistake? (The ball must land in the square in which the player is standing).
- Vary the size of the square according to the players' ability.
- Practice different techniques: passing, lobbing.

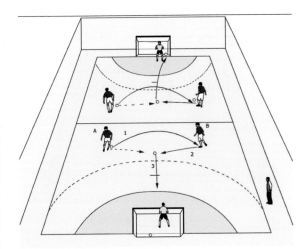

Ball Control – Goal!

Emphasis: Passing, scoring.

Equipment: Balls, 2 goals.

Set-up: Whole hall.

Implementation: Player A lobs the ball to player B, who controls the ball and passes it to A who is running towards the ball and then shoots at the goal. The players swap positions.

Duration: Unspecified.

Alternative: Play as a team game: which team scores the most goals in 10 attempts?

4.4.2 Small-sided games and training games

3 v 1

Emphasis: Passing.

Equipment: 2 balls (have other balls ready to avoid breaks in play), 8 cones, bibs.

Set-up: Mark out two 11 x 11 yard pitches in the hall.

Implementation: Play 3 v 1. The outside players should move out of the defender's 'shadow' so that they always have the option of passing to two players. If an outside player plays a bad pass or the defender wins the ball, they swap positions.

Duration: Unspecified.

Alternatives:

- Encourage direct play
- Two ball contacts per outside player
- Only pass the ball with the 'weak' foot.

3 v 3 + 1

Emphasis: Passing.

Equipment: 2 balls (have other balls on hand to avoid breaks in play), cones, bibs.

Set-up: Mark out 2 approx. 9 x 16 yard pitches with cones.

Implementation: Play 3 v 3 + 1: the team in possession of the ball plays with a 'joker' against 3 defenders. The joker team tries to obtain as many ball contacts as possible. Change roles if the defending team wins the ball.

Duration: Unspecified.

Alternative: Limit the number of ball contacts for the players on the team in possession of the ball. 5 ball contacts = 1 goal, after 5 goals, the losers have to carry out a funny forfeit.

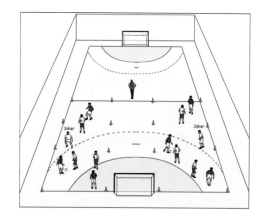

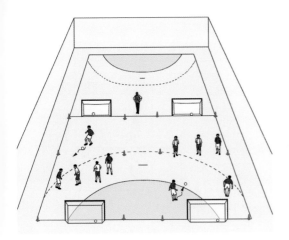

Three Contacts

Emphasis: Passing, scoring.

Equipment: 2 balls (have other balls on hand to avoid breaks in play), 10 cones, 4 goals (goal frame, if possible), bibs.

Set-up: Mark out 2 pitches, one in each half of the hall with a gap between them.

Implementation: Play 3 v 2 without a goal-keeper. The three players of the attacking team try to score a goal against 2 defenders. They have only three ball contacts and must only shoot at the goal from the opposing team's half of the pitch. The two defenders can play freely and may shoot at the goal from anywhere on the pitch.

Duration: Unspecified, but team composition should be changed frequently.

Alternatives:

- Time limit for the attackers
- Which team of 3 can score the most goals in 5 minutes?
- Which team of 2 can score the most goals in 5 minutes?

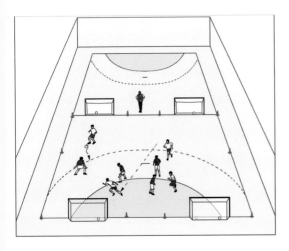

Double Kick

Emphasis: Dribbling, passing, scoring.

Equipment: Balls, 4 goals, cones, bibs.

Set-up: Mark out a playing area with 4 goals (goalframes if possible) on half a pitch.

Implementation: Play 4 v 4 into 4 goals. Each team must defend 2 goals and attack 2 goals.

Duration: 4 minutes – rest – coach briefing – 4 minutes, etc.

Alternative: Each team has two goals diagonally opposite each other.

1-1-2-1 System

Emphasis: Dribbling, passing, scoring.
Equipment: Balls, 2 goals, 6 cones, bibs.
Set-up: Mark out an approx. 11 x 22 yard pitch.
Implementation: Play 5 v 5 in a reduced space. Two teams play each other in 1-1-2-1 formation. The coach intervenes to encourage offensive and defensive play.
Duration: Unspecified.
Alternative: Watch out for long balls!

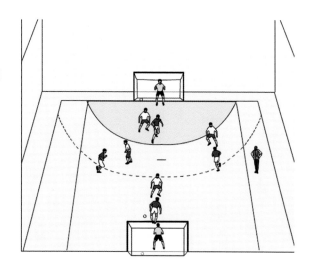

Joker

Emphasis: Dribbling, passing, scoring.
Equipment: Balls, 2 goals, bibs.
Set-up: Half the hall, divide the group into teams.
Implementation: Play 4 v 4 +1 (joker). The team in possession of the ball plays with the joker. If the defending team wins the ball, this team now plays with the joker and tries to score a goal. The scoring team retains possession of the ball.
Duration: Unspecified.

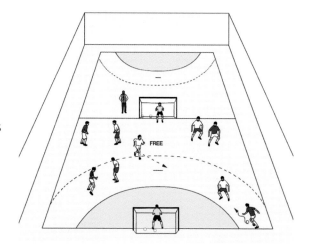

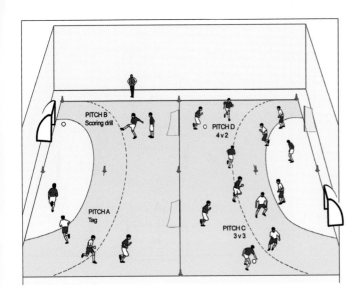

4 Stations
Emphasis: General training games.
Equipment: Balls, 11 cones, 12 posts with stand (or small goals), bibs, goals.
Set-up: Whole hall, mark out 4 pitches of about 11 x 22 yards.
Implementation:
Pitch A = tag.
Pitch B = scoring drill.
Pitch C = play 3 v 3.
Pitch D = play 4 v 2.
Duration: Unspecified.

Alternative: After a certain time, groups move round the stations in a clockwise direction.

Cone Goal Kick
Emphasis: Kicking.
Equipment: Balls, cones.
Set-up: Mark out two 16 x 11 yard pitches across the hall. Divide the group into appropriate teams.

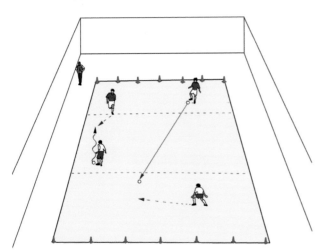

Implementation: Play with 4 players per pitch. 2 players try to kick the ball at the opposing team's cones. The player with the ball should dribble to the center and then shoot at the goal. The player may not be tackled in the center zone.
Duration: Unspecified.
Alternative: Which team can hit the most cones in 5 minutes?

4.4.3 Basic tactical rules

4 v 4 to 4 Goals

Emphasis: Play shifting.

Equipment: 1 ball, 16 cones, bibs.

Set-up: Use the whole hall. Mark out 4 goals along each side of the hall.

Implementation: Play 4 v 4 to 4 goals: each team defends 4 goals and tries to score in 4 goals. Focus on movement without the ball, moving into a space to receive the ball, play shifting, communication between defenders, taking on and beating opponents. Goals can only be scored from the opposing team's half.

Duration: Unspecified.

Alternative: Goals following play shifting count double.

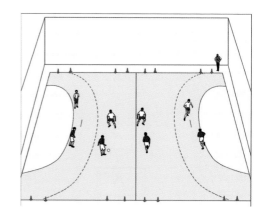

2 v 1 + Goalkeeper

Emphasis: Tactics.

Equipment: Balls, 2 goals, bibs.

Set-up: Whole pitch.

Implementation: Play 2 v 1 plus goalkeeper: a keeper rolls the ball to player A, who tries to outplay the defender with player B either by passing or by a feint in 1 v 1. The defender tries to disguise the passing path to delay the attack. Communication with the keeper is paramount.

Duration: Unspecified.

Alternatives:

- Shoot at the goal after 10 seconds.
- Which pair scores the most goals?
- Which defender wins the most balls?

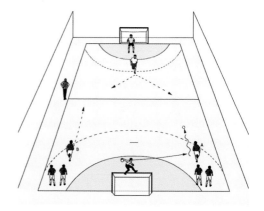

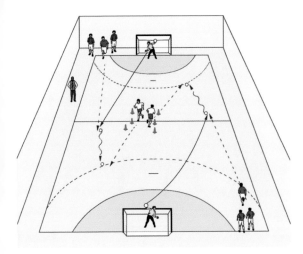

Goal Scoring under Opponent Pressure

Emphasis: Goal scoring.

Equipment: Balls, 2 goals, 6 cones.

Set-up: The whole pitch.

Implementation: 1 player from groups A and B sprints to the center line and runs to receive a ball thrown from the keeper. As soon as the players cross the center line they come under opponent pressure from behind. They then shoot at the goal under opponent pressure.

Duration: Unspecified.

Alternatives:

- Strikers from group A become defenders from group B and vice versa.
- Which group scores the most goals?
- Circuit (change defenders more often).

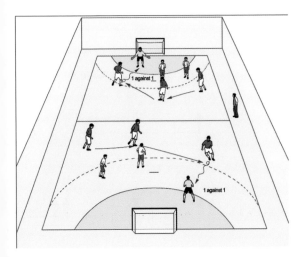

3 v 2 + Goalkeeper

Emphasis: Tactics.

Equipment: Balls, 2 goals, bibs.

Set-up: Play 2 games side-by-side in both halves of the pitch. Divide the players into appropriate groups.

Implementation: Play 3 v 2 + keeper. By clever play, the 2 defenders provoke a pass to the wing, thus creating a 3 x 1 on 1 situation. The keeper marks the player on the wing and takes over responsibility in the 1 on 1 situation.

Duration: Unspecified.

Alternative: Which team of 3 can score the most goals in 10 attempts? Then change teams around (attackers – defenders).

4.4.4   Conditioning drills

Sprint and Shoot!

Emphasis: Sprinting speed
Equipment: Balls, goal.
Set-up: Half pitch.
Implementation: Play 1 v 1. The coach stands on the center line between 2 groups. He passes the ball toward the goal and 2 players sprint after it. The first player shoots at the goal, the second retrieves the ball.
Duration: Unspecified.
Alternatives:

- Solid pairs – who scores the most goals?
- Start from different positions (sitting, lying down, squatting, etc.)

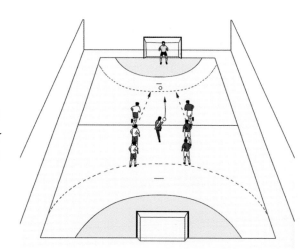

3 x 3 v 3 with 4 Goals

Emphasis: Conditioning.
Equipment: Ball, 8 cones, bibs.
Set-up: Mark out a pitch using 4 cones. Form 3 teams of 3.
Implementation: 3 x 3 v 3 with 4 goals. The coach keeps the ball in play. The team that receives the ball tries to score in 1 of the 4 goals.
Duration: Unspecified.
Alternative: Vary the size of the pitch.

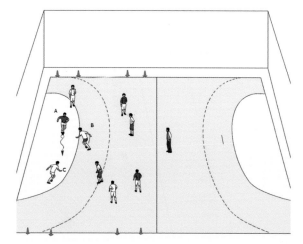

2 x 3 v 3

Emphasis: Conditioning.

Equipment: Ball, 4 cones, bibs.

Set-up: Mark out a 16 x 16 yard pitch. Form 3 teams of 3.

Implementation: 2 teams of 3 play against another group of 3, creating a 6 v 3 situation. The 6 players pass the ball to each other and try to keep the team of 3 in the center for as long as possible. If they lose the ball, the entire team of the player who lost the ball moves into the center.

Duration: Unspecified.

Alternatives:

*   Which team goes into the center least often?
*   Which team of six has most contact with the ball?

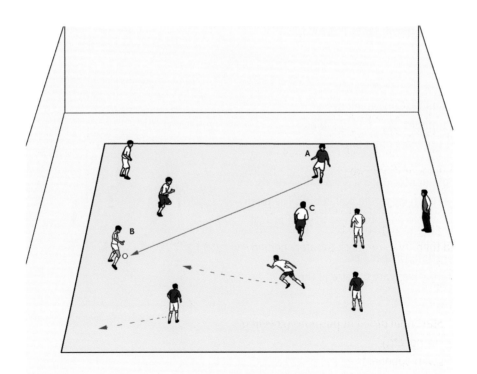

4.4.5 Conditioning

Feint and Score

Emphasis: Dribbling, passing, scoring.
Equipment: Balls, goal, 5 cones.
Set-up: Half a pitch.
Implementation: Player A dribbles around the cones and passes the ball to player B on the center line. B passes again to A, who then passes back to B. Player B dribbles toward the (partially active) defender, feints and shoots at the goal.
Duration: Unspecified.
Alternatives:

* Defenders are more active
* Work on specific feints.

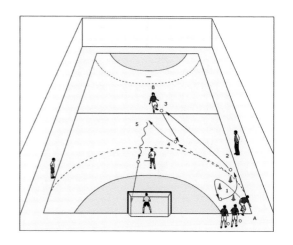

Nabbing

Emphasis: Coordination.
Equipment: None required.
Set-up: The whole hall, two groups.
Implementation: Two groups stand facing each other on the center line. The players in group A hold their arms out to the side. The players in group B touch their hands and then try to run back to safety behind the 7 yard line.
Duration: Unspecified.
Alternatives:

* Start from different positions (kneeling, sitting, etc.)
* Swap opponents.

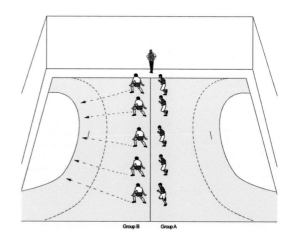

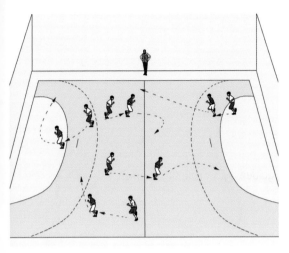

Shadow Running

Emphasis: Coordination.

Equipment: None required.

Set-up: The whole hall, divide players into pairs.

Implementation: Player B runs behind player A and, like a shadow, has to copy all his movements, e.g. jumps, turns, forward rolls, etc.

Duration: Unspecified.

Alternatives:

* May also be performed with ball.
* Swap teams around.

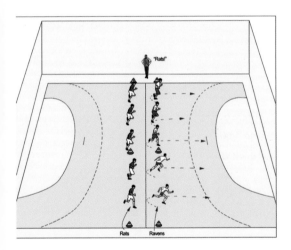

Rats and Ravens

Emphasis: Coordination.

Equipment: Bibs in 2 different colors, 6 cones.

Set-up: The whole hall, two groups.

Implementation: Two groups stand opposite each other on the center line about 3 yards apart. The players in the first group are the "rats" and in the second group the "ravens". When the coach calls "rats", this group must catch the "ravens"; when he calls "ravens", this group must catch the "rats". The caught players swap groups.

Duration: Unspecified.

Alternatives:

* Start from different positions (sitting, lying down, etc.)
* Start on a visual signal (raising a colored bib – red/yellow).

4.5   Training for 14-16 year-olds

Youngsters go through the so-called second pubertal phase between the ages of 14 and 16, and no longer want to be called or treated as children.

The phase is characterized by stagnation in height growth and an increase in width growth. This harmonizes the physical proportions, thus eliminating the coordinative problems that arose during the height growth spurt phase. Movement sequences become more rounded and the movement harmony of the golden age of learning returns.

That is why in this phase it makes sense to go back to working on coordination and technique, but now at a suitably higher intensity, to refine and deepen the basics that have already been learned. This is done using complex drills that should now be performed under time or accuracy pressure.

Furthermore, as befits the players' changed physical conditions, training is focused more and more on the development of conditioning skills, in particular by incorporating Futsal-specific strength and speed training into the drills. Acceleration drills and jumps combinations over boxes or partners can be integrated into some drills.

This makes the players' movements and actions more dynamic. The small teams in Futsal mean that for players the shift in conditioning load during matches resembles intensive interval training, meaning that speed endurance must be improved in training. This can be done particularly effectively in small-sided games. But also the targeted use of strength training can be a good idea at this age, in order to support the youngsters' width growth and to correct muscular imbalances.

There are other age-typical developmental milestones, as well as physical ones, that should be borne in mind for optimal training planning, i.e. improved concentration and balance, a certain psychological stability, increased self-confidence and last but not least a significant increase in motivation.

All these developmental milestones have a positive impact on the whole training process.

The coach can now work on training goals with his players that go beyond the mastery of Futsal-specific techniques.

This phase of the learning process is the time to further improve, deepen and consolidate the previously learnt tactical procedures (e.g. crossing in front of goal, running behind the ball, counter play, change of pace, etc). Game forms in which smaller teams play larger ones are particularly suited to this. Always keep score to make the drills more like a real game.

It is also now possible to focus on tactics that can be used in a match. Players in this age group are now capable of understanding connections and behaving rationally.

4.5.1 Basic technique drills

Dribbling Course

Emphasis: Dribbling, passing.

Equipment: Balls, 4 benches or box tops, cones.

Set-up: Whole hall.

Implementation: The player starts at the starting line, dribbles the ball, plays a one-two against the bench, then dribbles on to the next bench and plays another one-two. After controlling the ball, he dribbles through a slalom course to the opposite side, where he plays another two one-twos against two benches and dribbles over the finish line.

Duration: Unspecified.

Alternatives:

- Time the course.
- Play one-twos with the inside and outside of the feet.
- Start at the finish line in order to train both feet (right/left).

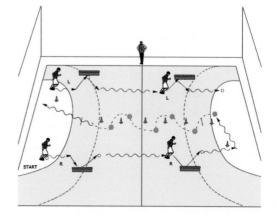

Triangle Passes

Emphasis: Dribbling, passing.

Equipment: Balls, cones.

Set-up: Mark out half a pitch with cones and place more cones randomly on the pitch (two playing areas fit into one pitch).

Implementation: Player A dribbles the ball and passes to player B. B traps the ball with the sole of the shoe, dribbles up to a cone, feints and passes to player C. C traps the ball with the sole of the shoe, dribbles up to a cone, feints and passes to A.

Duration: Unspecified.

Alternative: Swap round the teams of 3 so that partners are always changing.

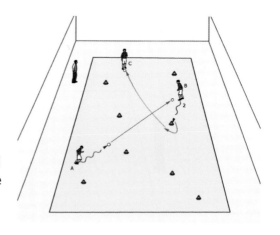

Scoring Game

Emphasis: Scoring.

Equipment: Balls, 4 bibs or hoops, cones.

Set-up: Fix bibs or hoops in the top corners of 2 goals.

Implementation: A player kicks using his toe from the 9 yard-line aiming at the bibs/hoops. Other players stand in or near the goal and roll the balls back. Players juggle the ball while waiting to shoot at the goal.

Duration: Unspecified.

Alternatives:

- Keep individual scores.
- Keep team scores (3 or more players).
- Keep pair scores. Who can score the most goals?

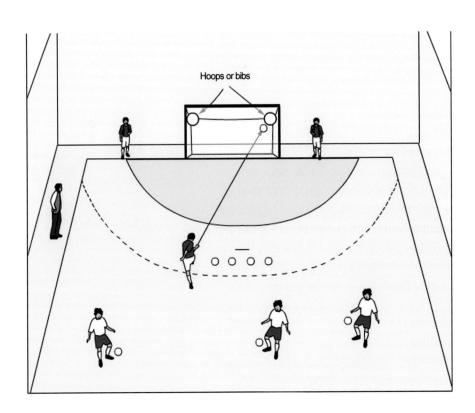

Hoops or bibs

4.5.2 Small-sided games and training games

Spin Kick King

Emphasis: Passing.

Equipment: Balls, 8 cones per pitch, 6 small cones.

Set-up: Mark out a 16 x 16 yard pitch (2 pitches are better to ensure that more players are active at the same time).

Implementation: Player A 'bends' the ball around the small cones through the goal on the opposite side to player B. B plays a straight pass to player C, who in turn plays a curved pass to player D. D then plays a straight pass to player A.

Duration: Unspecified.

Alternatives:

* Vary the size of the goals.
* Play in the other direction, kicking all passes with the left foot.
* Competition: change positions after three rounds. Who scores the most goals?

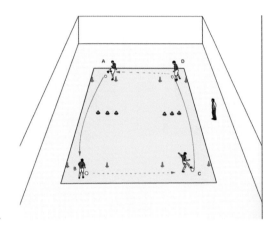

Overlap Attack

Emphasis: Dribbling, passing.

Equipment: Balls, 1 goal, 4 cones.

Set-up: Half a pitch, divide players into pairs.

Implementation: Two attackers start to play 2 v 1. If the attackers can outplay the defender, the ball-carrying player plays 1 v 1 against the second defender into two small cone goals. If the first defender manages to win the ball, he plays into the goal with a goalkeeper at the opposite end of the pitch.

Duration: Unspecified.

Alternative:

* The two defenders form a team and the two attackers form a team.
* Which team scores the most goals? Each team has 5 attempts each.

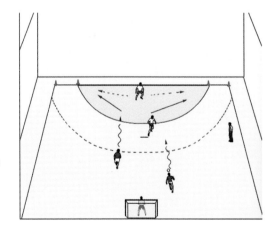

4 v 4 + 2

Emphasis: Dribbling, passing.
Equipment: Balls, bibs.
Set-up: Half a pitch.
Implementation: 4 v 4 +2: the team in possession of the ball plays 6 v 4 with two neutral players.
Duration: Unspecified.
Alternatives:

- The neutral players don't return the ball to the same players.
- Limit ball contact for the neutral players.
- Limit ball contact for the team in possession of the ball.
- After 10 contacts, the other team does e.g. 10 push-ups.

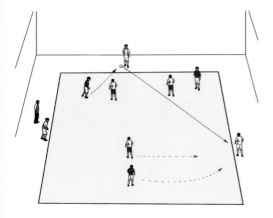

3 v 3 + 3

Emphasis: Dribbling, passing.
Equipment: Balls, cones, bibs.
Set-up: Mark out a 16 x 16 yard pitch with cones.
Implementation: Play 3 v 3 on the pitch. The team in possession of the ball is supported by 3 neutral players on the sidelines. The neutral players may only move along the lines.
Duration: Unspecified.
Alternatives:

- The team in possession of the ball should have a maximum of two contacts per player.
- Passing back to the same player is not allowed.
- After 10 contacts within the same team, a the neutral players swap places with one of the teams.

4.5.3 Basic tactical rules

Zone Defense

Emphasis: Tactics.

Equipment: Balls, 1 goal, 4 cones, bibs.

Set-up: Half a pitch, form two teams.

Implementation: Play 4 v 4 + keeper into two opposing goals. The coach encourages the defenders to defend the zones. Move to the ball. If the defenders win the ball, they try to score in the small cone goals on the center line opposite.

Duration: Unspecified.

Alternatives:

- Swap roles after 10 attacks.
- Which team scores the most goals?

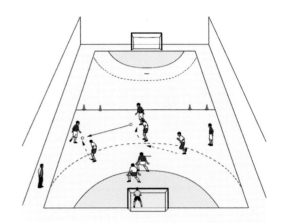

Free Game Build-up

Emphasis: Tactics.

Equipment: Balls, 2 goals, bibs.

Set-up: Whole pitch.

Implementation: Players 4 and 5 draw the goalkeeper wide. Player 3 remains in the center and monitors both sides. Players 4 and 5 move toward the ball-carrying player. Player 2 remains with the deepest attacker, the keeper moves forward.

Duration: Unspecified.

Alternatives:

- Many repetitions.
- Partially active defense.
- Free play after unchanging opening play.
- Change the teams around after 10 actions.

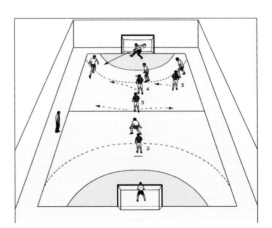

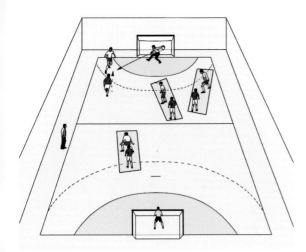

Man Marking

Emphasis: Tactics.

Equipment: Balls, 2 goals, bibs.

Set-up: Whole pitch.

Implementation: 4 x 1 v 1 = keeper. Fast ball capture by man marking over the whole pitch. Each player is responsible for one opponent.

Duration: At the coach's discretion, as this drill is very tiring.

Alternative: Which team scores the most goals?

Goals and Counter Goals

Emphasis: Tactics.

Equipment: Balls, 4 cones, 1 goal.

Set-up: Half a pitch, form two teams.

Implementation: Play 5 v 5. Play begins with a pass out to the left wing by player 1, followed by opponent pressure from A (pass along the line is blocked). B blocks the return pass, C moves into the center thus preventing a diagonal pass.
D remains in the center as long as possible. If ball possession is won, counter goals should be scored into the two small goals on the center line.

Duration: Unspecified.

Alternative: 10 opening plays. Which team scores the most goals?

Game with 1 Goal I

Emphasis: Tactics.

Equipment: Balls, 1 goal, bibs.

Set-up: Half a pitch, form teams.

Implementation: The game with one goal starts with a pass from 1 to 2. There are then 2 options for 2, depending on what the defender does next: pass to 3, who then passes to 4, pass to the approaching player B or pass to 3 who is running to the rear post. If the first pass from 2 to 3 is blocked, 2 passes to 4, thus enabling either a return pass or a square pass.

Duration: Unspecified.

Alternatives:

* Many repetitions.
* Defenders become increasingly active, the game is sped up.

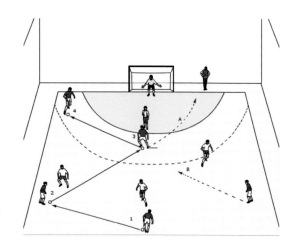

Game with 1 Goal II

Emphasis: Tactics.

Equipment: Balls, 1 goal, bibs.

Set-up: Player A breaks away from the defender with a deception and receives a pass from player B. Player A now passes the ball to player D. Player C crosses behind player A. Player D has the choice between passing to players A or C. The defenders are partially active. Players A or C attempt to score.

Duration: Unspecified.

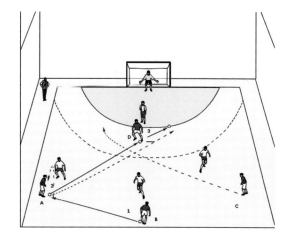

4.5.4 Conditioning drills

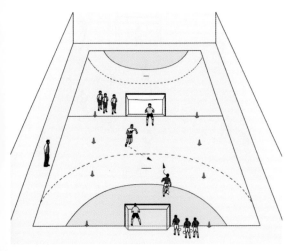

Corridor Game

Emphasis: Conditioning.

Equipment: Balls, 2 goals, bibs, 8 cones.

Set-up: Mark out an 11-yard-wide corridor with the cones in one half of a pitch. Form two teams.

Implementation: lay 1 v 1 in the 11-yard-wide corridor. The group that scores a goal then starts another game with the ball, otherwise just keep alternating ball possession.

Duration: 1 minute per 1 v 1.

Alternative: Which team scores the most goals?

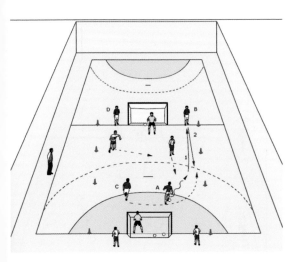

A/C with B/D

Emphasis: Conditioning.

Equipment: Balls, 2 goals, bibs, 8 cones.

Set-up: Mark out an 11-yard-wide corridor in one half of a pitch.

Implementation: A+C play together, B+D stand near the goal behind the center line. The players in the pitch can play with their partners on the lines in order to score a goal.

Duration: Not longer than 4 minutes per game.

Alternatives:

- Continuously change the composition of the teams
- Which team scores the most goals?
- Pass with 1 (2) touch(es)
- Don't pass back to the player who passed to you.

5 v 5 with Cone Goals

Emphasis: Conditioning.

Equipment: Balls, 12 (or more) cones, bibs.

Set-up: Half or whole pitch.

Implementation: 5 v 5 to several small goals spread over the pitch.

Duration: Unspecified.

Alternatives:

- Goals are valid only if a teammate receives the ball behind the cone goal.
- Goals scored after dribbling count double.
- Goals scored after a one-two count double.

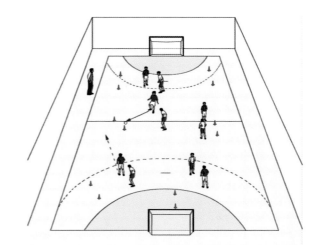

Cone Slalom

Emphasis: Conditioning.

Equipment: Balls, 2 goals, 10 cones.

Set-up: Whole pitch; divide the players into 2 groups.

Implementation: Both groups start at the same time: player A passes the ball to player B and sprints through the cone slalom. B plays a pass into A's path, who shoots at the goal. After this shot at the goal, A and B swap roles and player B sprints to the group.

Duration: Unspecified.

Alternative: Competition: Which group scores the most goals?

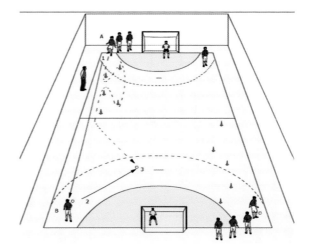

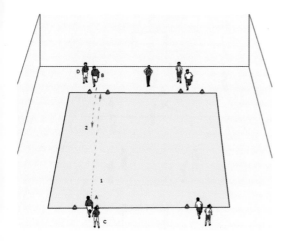

Shuttle Relay

Emphasis: Conditioning.

Equipment: Balls, 8 cones or posts with stand.

Set-up: Vary pitch dimensions and distances as required, divide players into teams.

Implementation: Two groups carry out a shuttle relay.

Duration: Unspecified.

Alternatives:

- Without ball.
- With ball.
- Carry the ball and give it to the next player at the hand-over.
- Dribble with one ball and carry another.
- Several relay runs may be carried out (e.g. each player runs 3 times).

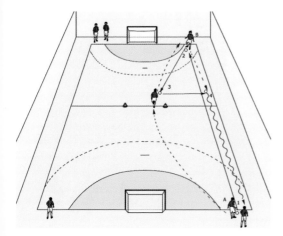

Sprint and Dribble

Emphasis: Conditioning.

Equipment: Balls, 2 posts with stand or 2 cones.

Set-up: Whole pitch, divide players into 2 groups.

Implementation: Player A passes the ball to the opposite side to player B and sprints to the post/cone on the center line. Player B plays a one-two with Player B and dribbles the ball to the starting corner, A sprints to collect the ball in the corner of the pitch.

Duration: Unspecified.

Alternatives:

- Each player starts 10 times (depending on requirements).
- Set the drill up on both sides of the pitch to practice kicking with right and left feet.

4.5.5 Coordination

Handball

Emphasis: Coordination.
Equipment: Balls, 4 cones, bibs.
Set-up: Mark out a pitch approx. 16 x 16 yards (11 x 11 yards), form 2 teams.
Implementation: The team in possession of the ball tries to touch the ball as many times as possible. Each player should keep the ball for no more than 3 seconds (3 steps). After 10 contacts, the other team performs a 'forfeit'. The ball may only be caught in the air.
Duration: Unspecified.
Alternative: The ball should not be thrown back to the passer (look for a 3rd player).

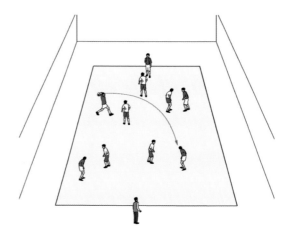

Handball Futsal

Emphasis: Coordination.
Equipment: Balls, 2 goals, bibs.
Set-up: Whole pitch, form 2 teams.
Implementation: 2 teams play handball against each other. Players should not keep the ball for longer than 3 seconds (3 steps). Goals may only be scored by volleys from the hand.
Duration: Unspecified.
Alternative: Goals may only be scored with the head.

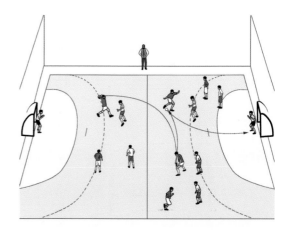

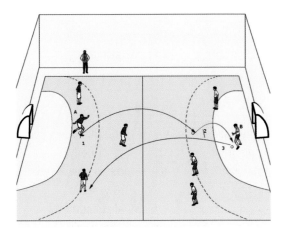

Volley Futsal
Emphasis: Coordination.

Equipment: Balls, bibs.

Set-up: Whole pitch, form 2 teams.

Implementation: Each team owns one half of the pitch. One player serves the ball from his hand in an arc into the other half of the pitch. The ball should bounce once and must then be kicked. After the third ball contact (at most), the ball must be kicked back into the other half.

Duration: Play to a time limit or for points (as desired, or 15 points).

Alternatives:
- Swap service after 5 serves.
- Whoever scores, serves.
- Serve from where the ball is.

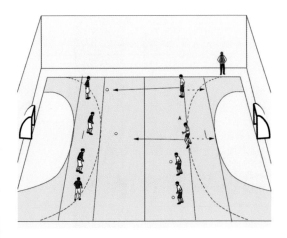

Strike!
Emphasis: Coordination.

Equipment: Balls, bibs.

Set-up: Whole hall, pitch from the 7 yard line to the 7 yard line, form 2 teams.

Implementation: Two teams stand facing each other. All the players on one team each have a ball. They try to throw the ball so that it hits their opposite number on the other side of the pitch. If they succeed, the hit player is out, if the ball is caught, the thrower is out.

Duration: When one team has no players left in, it has lost.

4.6   Training for 16-18 year-olds

The significantly increased motivation of the previous age group is now combined with a significantly increased physical performance, coupled with a more mature personality. The teen is now an **adolescent.**

The body reaches physical maturity during the teenage transition to adulthood, occasionally even continuing into the 20s. The culmination of this maturing of body and mind naturally has implications for training content and form. The time is now right for performance-oriented, adult training. The physical resilience of an 18-year-old player already corresponds to that of an adult, except in the areas of maximal strength and speed endurance, where longer recovery breaks are necessary due to the teen's smaller energy reserves.

Because of the muscle structure of 16-18 year-olds, the training structure significantly affects the attainable speed and speed strength levels in adulthood. This should be exploited with an appropriate training structure, which concerns not only the loading breaks within a training session but also the breaks between the training sessions over the course of a week or longer period of time.

As well as a polished technique, speed is one of the most important parameters of Futsal-specific performance. As modern Futsal becomes ever faster and more dynamic, the demands on players' speed skills are also increasing. What use is the fastest sprinting speed though if a player is not able to implement it intelligently during a game?

Training should therefore be structured so that the different speed components (acceleration, movement speed) are never practiced in isolation but are always integrated. Good basic speed is only useful when combined with an appropriate technique. This is why the refining and consolidating of technique is also very important in this age group.

Technique training initially takes place in drills with a high number of repetitions. These drills ingrain and make individual movement sequences automatic. All drills should therefore be performed with both feet. The disadvantage of these drills is the lack of connection of the movement to a complex match-specific situation, which is why game forms still form the core of technique training. This is the only way to enable players to solve even difficult match situations flexibly and successfully by learning to act effectively.

In the structure of this long-term training process, in the previous developmental phase, players were taught a wide spectrum of individual and group tactical options. Now the focus is on tactical specialization. The individual strengths and qualities of a player that have been developed in the first training phases now determine which position he plays and his role within the team. These positive qualities are now further honed, developed and reinforced in training.

4.6.1 Basic technique drills

Lob – Shoot

Emphasis: Scoring.

Equipment: Balls, goal, 6 cones.

Set-up: Half a pitch, divide the players into 2 groups.

Implementation: Player A passes the ball to player B and runs to the cone in front of him, around it, receives a high lob from B into the marked area then shoots at the goal.

Duration: Unspecified.

Alternatives:

- Practice from both sides; shoot with right and left feet.
- Each player must carry out 5 shots. Who scores the most goals?

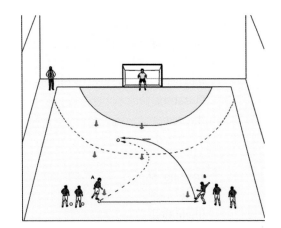

Lob – Stop – Shoot

Emphasis: Scoring.

Equipment: Balls, 1 (2) goal(s).

Set-up: Half a pitch – 11-16 yards in front of the goal. Tip: use both goals to keep players moving.

Implementation: A group of players (A) stands about 11-16 yards in front of the goal on one sideline. A player (B) stands about 5.5 yards in front of the group and another player (C) in the center of the pitch. A lobs over B to C who controls the ball then shoots at the goal. Player A then goes to position C, C to B and B to A.

Duration: Unspecified.

Alternatives:

- Practice from both sides; shoot with right and left feet.
- Vary ball control: chest, thigh, instep.

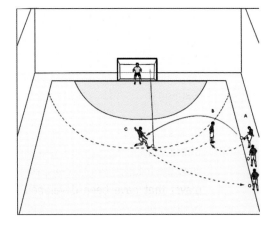

Header Monster

Emphasis: Heading.

Equipment: Balls, 2 goals, 5 cones.

Set-up: Half a pitch, divide the players into 2 groups.

Implementation: One player from each team stands inside the cone triangle and receives a ball thrown high over the goal by a player on his team. He heads the ball into the goal and swaps positions with the thrower who becomes the header, etc.

Duration: Unspecified.

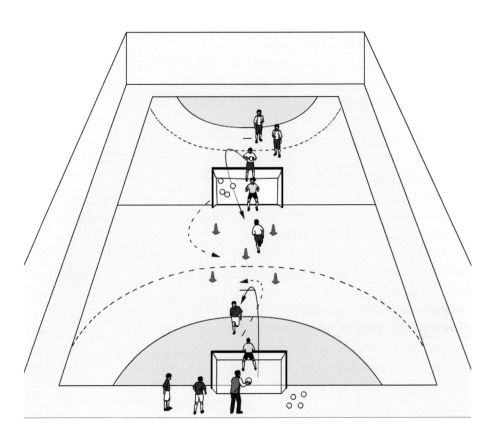

4.6.2 Small-sided games and training games

From 1 v 1 to 4 v 4

Emphasis: Small-sided games.
Equipment: 4 balls, 20 cones, bibs.
Set-up: Play across the pitch.
Implementation: Initially, play in parallel 1 v 1 with two small cone goals. Then two pitch boundaries are removed and the players play 2 v 2 on one half of the pitch with 4 small cone goals. Then play 4 v 4 with 8 small goals using the whole pitch.
Duration: Play to a time limit (1-2 mins), later for points (the winner is the first to score 10 goals).

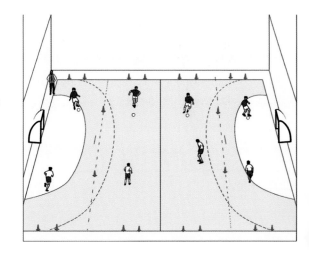

Tackle

Emphasis: Small-sided games.
Equipment: Balls, 6 cones, bibs, 2 goals.
Set-up: Play in a corridor in one half of the hall. Divide players into 2 teams.
Implementation: The teams stand near their goal. As soon as the coach puts the ball in play, the first players in each group start off and play 1 v 1 into the opposite goal.
Duration: Unspecified.
Alternative: Competition – Which team is first to score 10 goals?

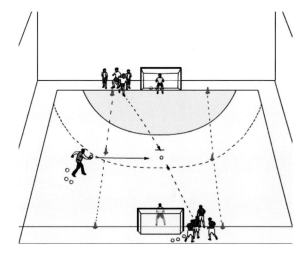

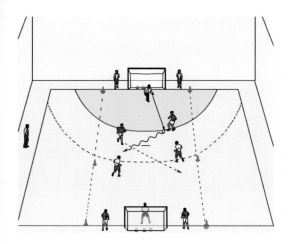

Deep Passes

Emphasis: Small-sided games.

Equipment: Balls, 6 cones, bibs, 1 portable goal.

Set-up: Play on half a pitch. Divide players into 2 teams of 4.

Implementation: The keeper rolls the ball to one of his two teammates. They try to score a goal against 2 defenders. They are helped by 2 players near the opponents' goal who may only be DIRECTLY passed back to, though.

Duration: Play to a time limit or until one team has scored 10 goals.

Alternatives:

- Continuously switch roles.
- Change roles after 3 attacks.

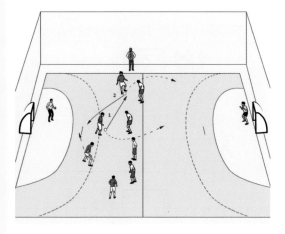

Pass and Sprint

Emphasis: Small-sided games.

Equipment: Balls, bibs, 2 goals.

Set-up: Use the whole pitch. Divide players into 2 teams.

Implementation: After each pass, the player must change position with a 5.5-yard sprint.

Duration: Play to a time limit or until one team scores 5 goals.

Alternatives:

- Free play.
- Each player can touch the ball no more than twice in each play.

5 + 2 against 5 + 2

Emphasis: Small-sided games.

Equipment: Balls, bibs, 2 goals.

Set-up: Play on the whole pitch. Divide the players into 2 teams.

Implementation: 2 teams play 5 v 5 on the pitch. Both teams have 2 teammates on the opposing baseline who may be passed to but must then play on DIRECTLY.

Duration: Play to a time limit or until one team scores 10 goals.

Alternative: A goal scored directly after a return pass from the baseline counts double.

4.6.3 Basic tactical rules

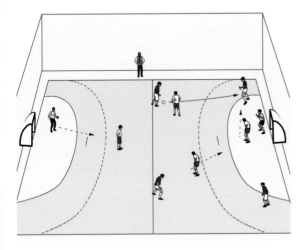

Emphasis: Basic tactical rules.
Equipment: Balls, bibs, 2 goals.
Set-up: Play on the whole pitch, form 2 teams.
Implementation: Play 5 v 5. The team without the ball may only defend with 3 players on the pitch, one teammate remains in the opposing team's half. If the ball is won by the defending team, it is immediately passed deep to the free teammate, thus switching to an attack.
Duration: Play to a time limit or until 1 team scores 10 goals.
Alternatives:
* Change roles continuously.
* Change roles after 10 attacks.

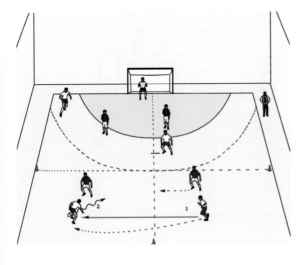

Emphasis: Basic tactical rules.
Equipment: Balls, cones, bibs, 1 goal.
Set-up: Play on half a pitch that is divided into 4 zones with cones. Form 2 teams.
Implementation: Play 4 v 4 into one goal. The 4 defenders may only defend in their own 'zone' and may not help out in another 'zone' in a 2 v 1 situation.
Duration: Play to a time limit or until 1 team scores 10 goals.
Alternatives:
* Change roles continuously.
* Change roles after 5 attacks.

3 v 3 with 4 Goals

Emphasis: Basic tactical rules.

Equipment: Balls, cones, bibs, small goals or goal frames.

Set-up: In each half of the hall, mark out a pitch about 11 x 16 yards (or 16 x 22 yards).

Implementation: In each half of the pitch, play 3 v 3 with 4 goals. Each team must defend 2 goals and attack 2 goals.

Duration: Play to a time limit or until 1 team scores 5 goals.

Alternatives:

- Play tournaments.
- All teams play each other.
- Set up a league table.

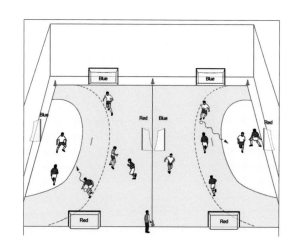

Chasing and Outnumbering

Emphasis: Basic tactical rules.

Equipment: Balls, bibs, 1 goal.

Set-up: Use the whole pitch.

Implementation: Play 4 v 4 + keeper. Play kicks off in the team's own half. Player A passes to player B, A chases B, B rolls the ball back to player A, A passes to C, who has free play.

Duration: Play to a time limit or until 1 team scores 5 goals.

Alternative:

- Change tasks continuously.
- Change tasks after 10 attacks.

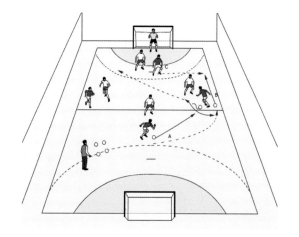

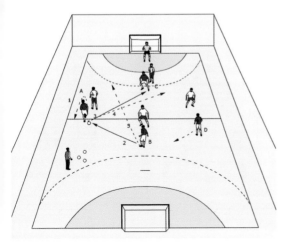

Outnumbering

Emphasis: Basic tactical rules.

Equipment: Balls, bibs, 1 goal.

Set-up: Use the whole pitch.

Implementation: Play 4 v 4 + keeper. Play kicks off in the team's own half. Player A starts with a running feint, then receives the ball from player B, A passes to player C, A and B run behind the pass thus outnumbering the other team. Player D remains at the back and moves to the center.

Duration: Play to a time limit or until 1 team scores 5 goals.

Alternatives:

- Change tasks continuously.
- Change tasks after 10 attacks.

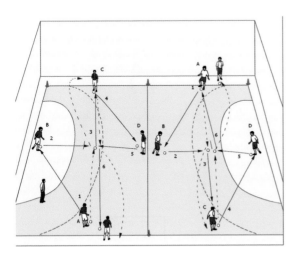

One-Two

Emphasis: Basic tactical rules.

Equipment: Balls, 6 cones.

Set-up: Use the whole pitch. Divide players into 2 teams.

Implementation: Use both halves of the pitch in parallel. A passes to B and runs into the center, B passes to A, A to C and runs back to the starting position. C passes to D and runs to the center, D to C, C to A and runs back to the starting position. After a few run-throughs, players A and C swap with B and D.

Duration: Play to a time limit or e.g. until 10 rounds are completed correctly.

Alternatives:

- Change direction.
- Practice with both left and right feet.

4.6.4 Conditioning drills

Kick and Run

Emphasis: Conditioning.

Equipment: Balls, 8 cones.

Set-up: Mark out a 16 x 16 yard pitch in each half of the hall. 2 groups work in parallel.

Implementation: Player A passes to player B, who passes back to A. Player A passes diagonally to player C and sprints to position B. After passing back to player A, player B runs around the cones and sprints to position C. Player C passes the ball back to position B (now occupied by player A), turns around the cone and sprints to D. Position B (= player A) passes diagonally to D.

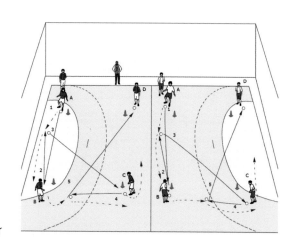

Duration: Play to a time limit or a certain number of rounds.

Alternative: Competition: Which group is first to complete 1 (3) round(s)?

Run – Jump – Volley

Emphasis: Conditioning.

Equipment: Balls, 4 gymnastic poles, 6 hoops, 2 goals.

Set-up: Use the whole hall. Divide the players into 2 teams.

Implementation: Player A passes the ball to player B, then sprints through the hoops, sprints to the goal area, receives the ball back from B and shoots at the goal. Player B takes the ball with him to the other group, player A takes over B's position and becomes the passer. The other group passes the ball to the coach, jumps over the posts, sprints to the goal area and plays a volley shot at the goal.

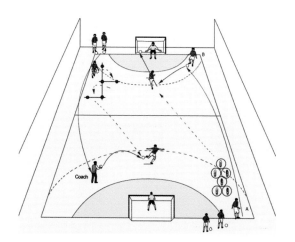

Duration: Play to a time limit or complete a certain number of rounds.

Alternative: Which player is first to score 5 goals?

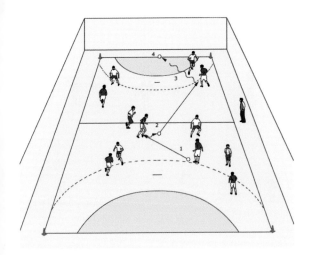

Line Futsal

Emphasis: Conditioning.

Equipment: Balls, 4 cones, bibs.

Set-up: Use the whole pitch. Form 2 teams of 6 players.

Implementation: Play 6 v 6 with line goals using the whole pitch.

Duration: Play to a time limit or until one team scores 10 goals.

Alternatives:

- Limit the number of ball contacts.
- Goals scored after dribbling count double.
- Goals scored after one-two count double.

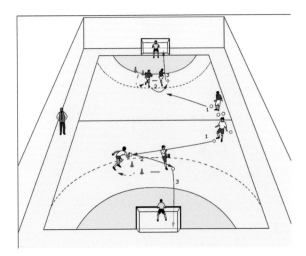

Goal Shooting Intervals

Emphasis: Conditioning.

Equipment: Balls, 4 cones.

Set-up: Work on both halves of the pitch in parallel. Divide the players into 2 groups.

Implementation: One player receives a powerful pass from the center line, starts from the cone goal then controls and runs with the ball before shooting at the goal.

Duration: Change after 5-10 repetitions.

Alternative: Train with the right and left feet.

Conditioning Kick

Emphasis: Conditioning.

Equipment: Balls, 8 cones.

Set-up: Use both halves of the pitch, divide the players into 2 groups.

Implementation: One coach and an assistant coach practice with one player. They throw or pass the ball freely into the marked pitch. The player passes the ball back to the passer.

Duration: Play to a time limit or after passing the ball back 10 times (Note: very intensive!).

Alternatives:

- Form several groups, the balls are then passed by teammates.
- Allow 2 ball contacts.
- Dribble briefly with the ball after receiving the pass.

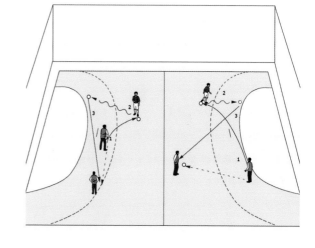

Tackle

Emphasis: Conditioning.

Equipment: Balls, bibs, 2 goals.

Set-up: Play on the whole pitch, form 2 groups.

Implementation: 4 pairs play 1 v 1 with keeper. The player who outplays his opponent runs alone to the opponent's goal and may not now be attacked.

Duration: Play to a time limit or until one team scores 5 goals.

Alternative: In another run-through, new pairs are formed to play 1 v 1.

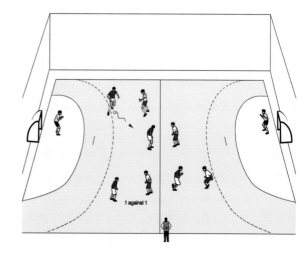

4.6.5 Coordination

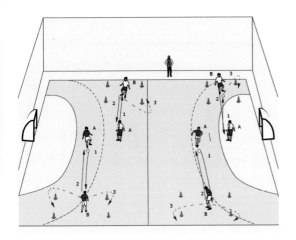

Cone Circuit

Emphasis: Coordination.

Equipment: Balls, 16 cones.

Set-up: Divide the players into 4 groups and use the whole pitch. Mark out 4 areas approx. 6 x 11 yards with cones.

Implementation: Player A passes to player B, who passes the ball back and sprints around a cone, then plays another one-two with player A before sprinting around the next cone, etc.

Duration: Play to a time limit or until 1 player has sprinted around all the cones or change after 10 one-twos.

Alternative: Competition: Who is first to sprint around all 4 cones?

Turning – Orientation

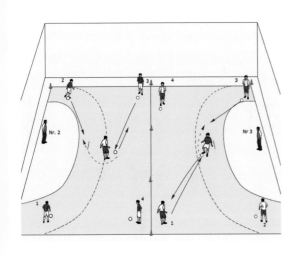

Emphasis: Coordination.

Equipment: 8 balls, 8 cones.

Set-up: Train on both halves of the pitch in parallel. Divide the players into 2 groups.

Implementation: 4 players with a ball each own a quarter of the pitch. The coach calls out a name (or a number), this player passes his ball to the player in the center of the pitch who passes the ball back, next pass, etc.

Duration: Play to a time limit or until 10 return passes. Then the next player goes into the center.

Alternatives:
* Perform the drill with reduced distances.
* Perform the drill with headers.

7 v 3

Emphasis: Coordination.

Equipment: Balls, 6 cones, bibs.

Set-up: Play on the whole pitch. Divide the players into 2 teams, one with 7 players and one with 3.

Implementation: The players in the group with 7 players pass the ball DIRECTLY to each other. The pass-giver must run around a cone after passing the ball but he is not allowed to chose the cone nearest to him. If a defender intercepts the ball, he swaps places with the pass-giver.

Duration: Play to a time limit or until one team has passed the ball 10 times without making a mistake.

Alternative: Two ball contacts are allowed.

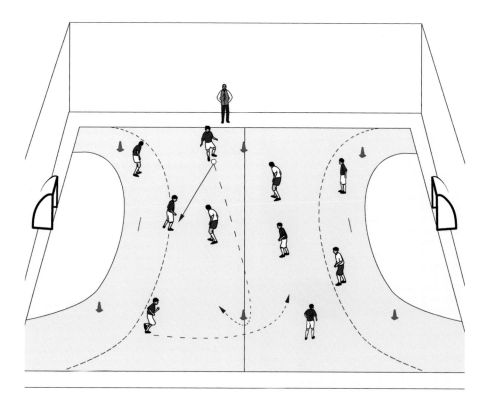

4.7 Training for over-18 year-olds (seniors)

The players now play against each other in weekly league matches and their playing level is now almost the same. The differences are much smaller than in youth soccer, so it is therefore difficult to give one's own team an advantage with targeted, intensive technique training. However, a difference can be made with the performance-influencing factors action speed and the players' physical and mental qualities. An improvement in these parameters leads to a faster, more dynamic game and so to all-important victories!

Because usually there are only a few training sessions available per week, the question is how all this can be fit in. Even conditioning can be trained effectively in a game-specific format. Conditioning training can be match-oriented by combining it with other elements from the areas of technique and tactics. This motivates the players while improving their game. Of course, in certain phases of the mastery/championship, the isolated training of speed, speed strength and strength endurance is still appropriate, although fundamentally training should be match-oriented.

As everybody knows, matches are the best training!

4.7.1 Basic technique drills

Handball – Header – Goal!
Emphasis: Basic techniques.
Equipment: Balls, 2 goals, bibs.
Set-up: Half a pitch, divide players into 2 groups.
Implementation: Play handball 5 v 5. Goals may only be scored by heading the ball after it has been passed. Players may not run with the ball and not keep it for more than 3 seconds. Passes from the keeper are also allowed.
Duration: Unspecified.
Alternative: Goals can also be scored with the feet after a throw from a teammate (volley).

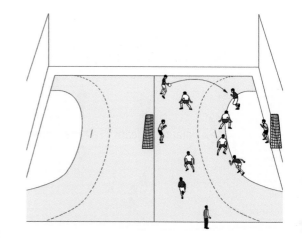

Dribbling – Lob
Emphasis: Dribbling, ball control.
Equipment: Balls, bibs.
Set-up: Whole pitch, form teams of 2, 1 ball per pair.
Implementation: The players with the ball dribble freely on the pitch. Then the player lobs the ball to his teammate, who controls the ball, dribbles for a while and then lobs the ball back.
Duration: Unspecified.
Alternatives:
- Start the drill on an acoustic or visual signal from the coach.
- The ball is kicked instead of lobbed to the teammate.
- Stop the ball with the chest.
- Mix up the teams a few times.

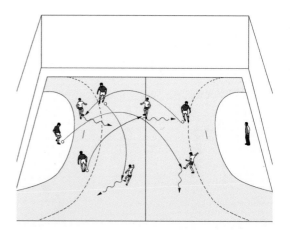

4.7.2 Small-sided games and training games

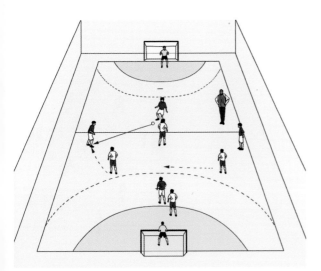

Defend the Diamond

Emphasis: Passing, positional play.

Equipment: Balls, bibs.

Set-up: Whole pitch, divide the players into 2 teams.

Implementation: The players of both teams stand in a diamond formation in which they try to intercept the ball. The players defend 'their' area. Follow the coach's advice!

Duration: Unspecified.

Alternative: Quick switch from defense to offense after winning the ball.

Pressing Forward

Emphasis: Defensive play.

Equipment: Balls, bibs.

Set-up: Whole pitch, players are divided into 2 teams.

Implementation: The players start to attack the opposing team in their half in order to gain possession of the ball as quickly as possible.

Duration: About 4 minutes per game – rest – etc.

Alternative: Other tactical tasks possible.

Uneven Game Situation

Emphasis: Passing and running into a space.

Equipment: Balls, bibs.

Set-up: Whole pitch, players are divided into 2 teams.

Implementation: Player A passes the ball left to player B and runs down the center of the pitch. Player B passes to player C and runs down the line behind the defender. Player C now has 2 options: one-two with player B or pass to player A. Player D provides back-up.

Duration: Unspecified.

Alternative:

- Practice on both sides (left/right)
- Players change positions and tasks.

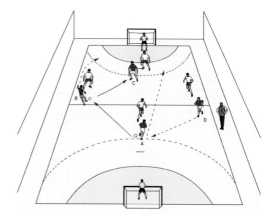

Quick Switch

Emphasis: Sprinting, dribbling, scoring.

Equipment: Balls, bibs, 4 cones.

Set-up: Whole pitch, players are divided into attackers and defenders.

Implementation: Two attackers stand on the outside lines, a defender on the 7-yard line. The keeper throws (rolls) the ball right or left into the path of an attacker. The defender sprints behind the attacker and the attacker tries to score a goal as quickly as possible.

Duration: Unspecified.

Alternative: Form 2 teams, the winner is decided after each team has carried out 10 attacks.

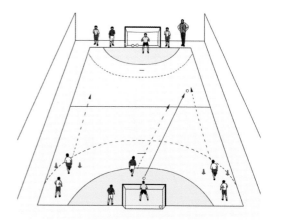

Goalkeeper as Defender

Emphasis: Overlap attack.

Equipment: Balls, bibs.

Set-up: Train in parallel on both halves of the pitch, players are divided into 2 groups.

Implementation: Play 3 v 2 + 1 (keeper). Three attackers play against two defenders + keeper into one goal. The defenders shift the game so as to provoke a 1 v 1 situation between a forward and a goalkeeper.

Duration: Unspecified.

Alternative: To finish, both training groups play each other 6 v 6.

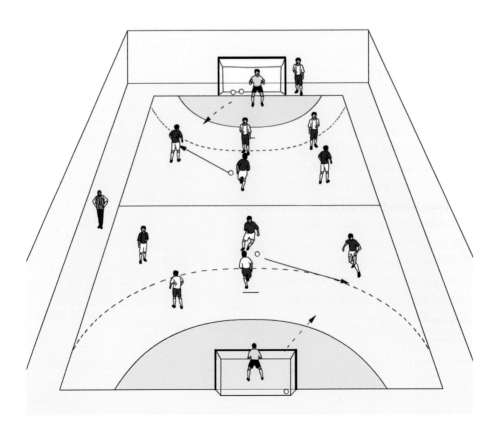

4.7.3 Basic tactical rules

Fast Attack after Goal Throw
Emphasis: Tactics.
Equipment: Balls, bibs.
Set-up: Whole pitch, players are divided into teams.
Implementation: 3 pairs stand in a 1 v 1 situation in one half of the pitch, 1 pair stands in the other half of the pitch near the sidelines (in order to draw out the defenders). The keeper holds the ball, one player from the attacking team moves out of his own half, the keeper throws the ball into his path, thus creating a 2 v 1 (+ keeper) situation in front of the opposing team's goal.
Duration: Unspecified.
Alternatives:
- Each team has 10 chances to attack.
- Who can score the most goals?
- The two teams then play a 5 v 5game against each other.

Opening Play
Emphasis: Tactics.
Equipment: Balls, bibs.
Set-up: Whole pitch, players are divided into 2 teams.
Implementation: The keeper rolls the ball to player A, who plays a one-two with player B, while simultaneously player C start to run down the sideline, creating a passing opportunity with his sprint. Player A passes the high ball into the path of C, thus creating a 2 v 1 situation with players C and D against one defender (+ keeper).
Duration: Unspecified.
Alternatives:
- Each team has 10 attempts – who scores the most goals?
- Then the two teams play each other.

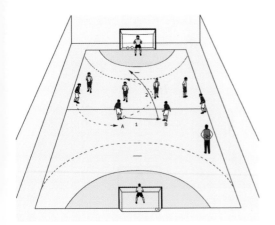

Through the Gap

Emphasis: Tactics.

Equipment: Balls, bibs.

Set-up: Whole pitch, players are divided into 2 teams.

Implementation: 4 pairs stand in a 1 v 1 formation on the center line. Player A passes to player B and starts to run diagonally but then stops and receives a flat pass from player B through the 'gap'. A then plays 1 v 1 against the keeper.

Duration: Unspecified.

Alternatives:

- Each team has 10 attempts: who scores the most goals?
- Followed by 5 v 5 game.
- Pass with a lob.

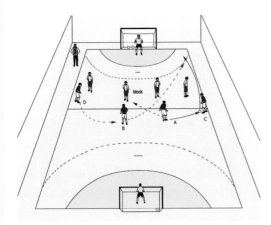

Blocking

Emphasis: Tactics.

Equipment: Balls, bibs.

Set-up: Whole pitch, players are divided into 2 teams.

Implementation: Player A passes the ball out to player C on the wing. In the center, players A + B form a 'block'. Player B runs diagonally in front of player A into the corner of the pitch, player A 'blocks' the player marking player B. Player C lobs the ball to player B. Player D returns to the center and now forms the 'block' with player A.

Duration: Unspecified.

Alternative:

- Practice on both sides.
- Each team has 10 attempts – who can score the most goals?
- Followed by a game between the 2 training groups.

Uneven-sided Game I

Emphasis: Tactics.

Equipment: Balls, bibs.

Set-up: Whole pitch, players are divided into 2 teams.

Implementation: One team makes a tactical swap of the goalkeeper for a fifth field player at a kick in to outnumber the opposite team:

Three players stand on the sideline facing the substitute's bench, another player moves in the opposite corner of the pitch. The keeper sprints off the pitch and is replaced by a fifth field player.

Duration: Unspecified.

Alternatives:

- Each team has 10 attempts – who can score the most goals?
- Finish with competitive game.

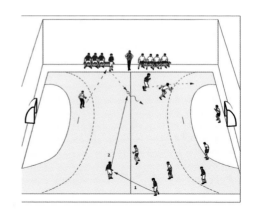

Uneven-sided Game II

Emphasis: Tactics.

Equipment: Balls, bibs.

Set-up: Whole pitch, players are divided into 2 teams.

Implementation: Play 5 v 4 + 1: one team has swapped their keeper for a player. This team has possession of the ball and stands in a 1-2-2 formation. The defending team stands in a diamond-formation. The coach specifies the type of attack required and the players try to implement this, here in training, later in a match.

Duration: Unspecified.

Alternatives:

- Each team has 10 attempts – who scores the most goals?
- Finish with competitive game.

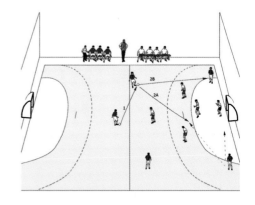

4.7.4 Conditioning drills

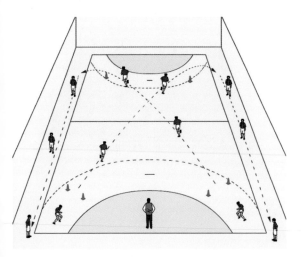

Diagonal Runs

Emphasis: Basic conditioning training.

Equipment: 6 cones.

Set-up: Whole pitch, players are divided into 2 groups.

Implementation: Both training groups start in parallel. At the starting cone, they carry out a pre-determined activity and start a diagonal run around the appropriate cone (80% intensity). They run back at a relaxed pace then start again.

Duration: Unspecified, depends on the training goal. Rest breaks are important!

Alternatives:

- Many low-intensity runs.
- A few high-intensity runs.

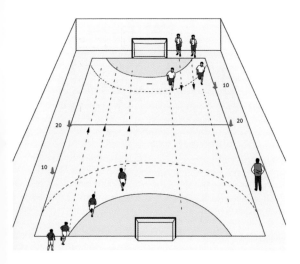

Sprint Training

Emphasis: Conditioning.

Equipment: 4 cones.

Set-up: Whole pitch, players are divided into 2 groups.

Implementation: Both groups start in parallel. The players sprint 11 yards on one side and 22 yards on the other side.

Duration: Depends on training goal. Rest breaks are important!

Alternatives:

- Run 11 yards on both sides.
- Run 22 yards on both sides.
- Alternate between the two.

Sprint Training with Ball and Final Shot at the Goal

Emphasis: Conditioning.

Equipment: Balls, 8 cones.

Set-up: Whole pitch, players are divided into 2 groups.

Implementation: Player A plays a one-two with player B and then passes to player C. Player C passes square to player A so he can shoot at the goal. Swap positions after a few repetitions.

Duration: Unspecified.

Alternative: Player A plays a one-two with player B, A passes to C, A takes B's position. B plays a one-two with C and shoots at the goal. B takes C's position, C runs with the ball to the other side.

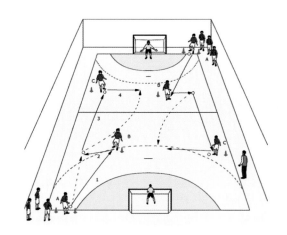

Game without Kick-in

Emphasis: Conditioning.

Equipment: Balls, bibs, 2 goals.

Set-up: Half a pitch, players are divided into 2 groups.

Implementation: 2 teams play 5 v 5. When the ball goes out, the team that would have kicked it in restart the game with a throw by their keeper. A very fast game that avoids long breaks.

Duration: Unspecified.

Alternatives:

• Play with or without corners.

• The losing team must perform an extra conditioning activity.

• Play several shorter games (e.g. up to 3 or 5).

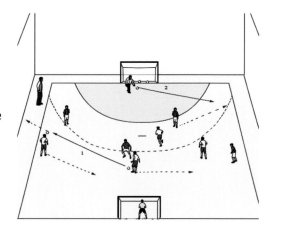

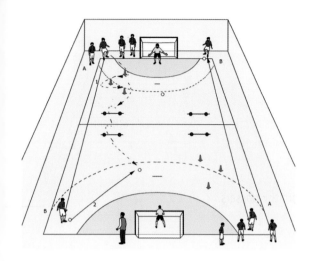

Slalom – Shoot
Emphasis: Conditioning.
Equipment: Balls, 6 cones, 4 x 2 hurdle cones with posts.
Set-up: Whole pitch, divide players into 2 groups, the groups work in parallel.
Implementation: Player A passes the ball to player B, then sprints through the cone slalom, jumps the hurdles, receives the ball passed by B and shoots at the goal. B retrieves the ball, then A takes over B's position.
Duration: Unspecified.
Alternativse
• Play to a time limit.
• Each player performs a certain number of circuits.

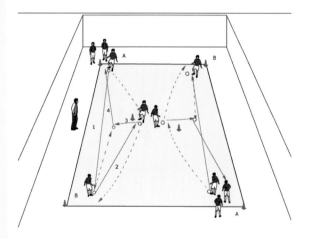

Pass and Sprint
Emphasis: Conditioning.
Equipment: Balls, cones.
Set-up: Mark out a pitch of about 13 x 16 yards, players are divided into 2 groups, the groups work in parallel.
Implementation: Player A passes the ball to player B. A sprints to the cone, B passes back to A, one-two, B runs with the ball to player A's starting point, A takes over B's position.
Duration: Unspecified.
Alternatives:
• Play to a time limit.
• Each player performs a certain number of circuits.

3 + 2 v 3 + 2

Emphasis: Conditioning, passing.

Equipment: Balls, 2 goals, bibs, cones.

Set-up: Half a pitch, players are divided into 2 groups.

Implementation: Two teams play 3 v 3 with keeper. Two other players on each team stand next to the opposing team's goal and act as passers for their teams. Goals can be scored by individual moves or with the help of the passers.

Duration: 2-3 minutes per game, several reps.

Alternatives:

* Goals may only be scored after a pass from the passers.
* The passers may only play direct passes.
* Goals may only be scored after a lob.

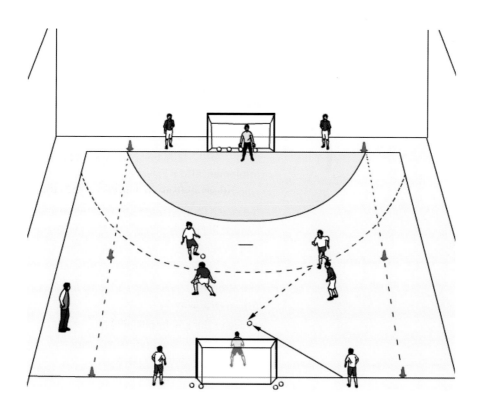

4.7.5 Coordination

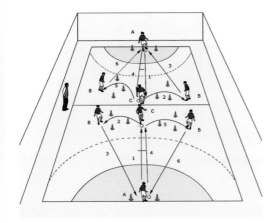

Emphasis: Coordination (lob).

Equipment: Balls, 16 cones.

Set-up: Mark out 2 pitches of 11 x 11 yards each, players are divided into 2 groups.

Implementation: Three players (A-B-B) stand in a triangle around player C. Player A passes to player C, who controls the ball and lobs over the cone to player B. He passes back to A and the drill starts again.

Duration: Each player 10 lobs (5 x right foot/5 x left foot).

Alternatives:

- May also be performed as a circuit.
- Several players stand at position A.

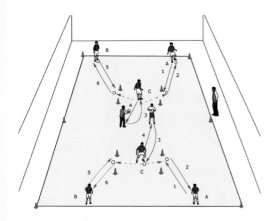

Heading/Passing

Emphasis: Coordination.

Equipment: Balls, cones.

Set-up: Mark out 2 pitches of 16 x 11 yards each, players are divided into 2 teams, both groups work in parallel.

Implementation: Player A passes to player C, who passes the ball back to A. C runs around the coach (player) and receives a throw to be headed, he heads the ball back, turns again and receives a pass from player B which he returns.

Duration: Swap positions after 10 headers.

Alternatives:

- Head the ball from standstill.
- Head the ball with run-up/jump.
- Pass the ball with both feet.
- Final game between both teams – headed goals count triple.

"Training Game"

Emphasis: Coordination.

Equipment: Balls, bibs.

Set-up: Whole pitch, players are divided into 2 teams (8 v 8, 9 v 9, 10 v 10).

Implementation: Two teams of at least 8 players each play each other. The large number of players in a small space encourages rapid thinking and play.

Duration: Unspecified.

Alternatives:

- Limit number of ball contacts.
- No passing back to the passer of the ball.
- Goals scored after dribbling or a one-two are more valuable.

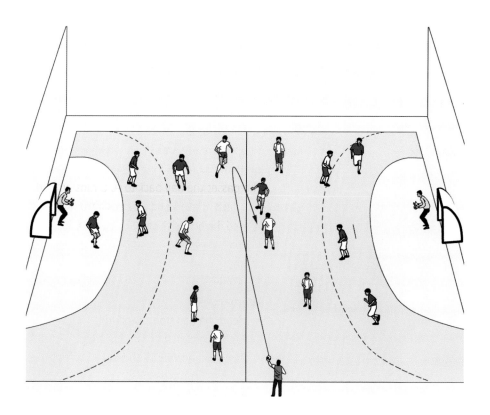

5 The Goalplayer

The Futsal goalkeeper must not only possess the same qualities as soccer or indoor soccer goalkeeper, he must also master special skills that are typical for the requirements of Futsal. In other words he must be a goal*player*, not just a goal*keeper*. He often initiates and participates in his team's attacks. Futsal's special rules call for additional qualities that often have decisive effect on the outcome of a match.

As scoring attempts into his goal often come from very close range, quick reactions (and courage) are essential. He must rush a fast-approaching attacker, is often confronted by an approaching striker who is free to shoot, or has to deal with dangerous action near the goal posts.

In order to defend the goal effectively, he must be able almost to 'read' the game:

* He must always keep his eye on the ball, particularly when the opposing team has possession of the ball and is preparing an attack.
* He must observe and anticipate the opponents' movements.
* He must organize his defense. As his position gives him the best overview of the events of the match he is ideally placed to guide his teammates.

The keeper is the 'ruler' of his penalty box! He should not act hesitantly but radiate strength and self-confidence to his teammates. A self-confident goalplayer gives his team support and rear cover!

The goalplayer's main task naturally consists of preventing goals. To this end it is necessary that he master two fundamental areas: positional play and goal defense.

The static position is a ready position; the keeper does not need to get directly involved in the events of the game, but observes the course of the game with concentration. In this position he is ready to move equally quickly to the left or to the right.

In dynamic positional play, the goalplayer does move; he is ready to play a direct part in the game and deliberately places his body between ball and goal. He either moves laterally or forwards, with the aim of shortening the angle between ball and goal. His arms should be held out to the side for stability and balance.

A shot at the goal can be defended in three different ways:

- The shot is parried and the ball is guided back into the pitch or behind the goal line.
- The ball is 'dampened' and controlled.
- The ball is caught.

As most shots on goal in Futsal are from a short range, and are therefore very fast, it is difficult for the goalplayer to catch the ball, so most of their actions involve simply clearing the ball to stop the opposing team from scoring.

If the shot comes from further away, or with less force, it is possible for the keeper to dampen the ball and let it drop, then control it and put it back in play immediately.

The safest method of defending a shot at the goal is to catch the ball, which usually only occurs when the ball is deflected or already dampened by a player, or if the shot comes from a great distance or was not kicked hard. If the goalplayer catches the ball, his team has an enormous tactical advantage as they can now set up a counterattack very quickly.

This is where the keeper's second important role in the game comes into play, i.e. as initiator of or participant in an attack. As soon as he has caught the ball, he is responsible for building up the attack: he either passes the ball to a nearby teammate or throws or kicks it to a forward in a promising position for a shot at the goal.

When the goalplayer controls the ball, he has the unique advantage of being able to put the ball back into play from a safe position and with a good overview of the game without pressure (apart from the 4 second rule). The ball is usually thrown accurately directly into the path of a teammate.

The goalplayer may sometimes find himself in the special situation of being used as a so-called 'flying goalkeeper'. However, this role is usually taken by an especially designated field player who also has the responsibilities of a keeper. The 'flying goalkeeper' is mostly used to reinforce attacking pressure.

Then he acts as a distributor in the midfield. Or it may be used just before the end of the match when the team wants to step up its attack to score an equalizer or improve a final score (the team has nothing to lose, as it were).

The following drills relate to the original tasks of a goalplayer, i.e. situational play and goal defense. There are no special, separate drills for a 'flying goalkeeper', as they are based on fieldplayers' drills.

Drills for the Goalplayer

Throwing Contest

Emphasis: Throwing.
Equipment: Balls, 2 goals, 4 cones.
Set-up: Set up 2 goals 16 yards apart in one third of the hall.
Implementation: Both goal players try to score a goal with a hard, accurate throw. They may only throw from the position in which they catch the ball and may not run with the ball!
Duration: Unspecified.

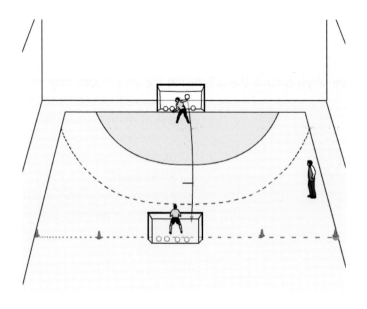

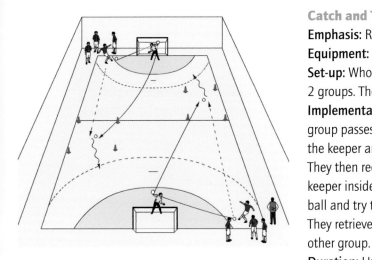

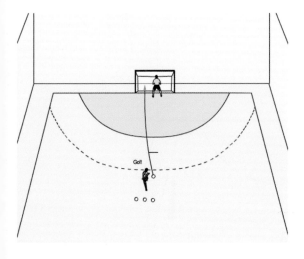

Catch and Throw!

Emphasis: Reactions and goal throw.
Equipment: Balls, 8 cones.
Set-up: Whole pitch, divide players into 2 groups. They work in parallel circuits.
Implementation: The first player in each group passes the ball into the hands of the keeper and sprints to the center line. They then receive the ball thrown by the keeper inside a marked area, control the ball and try to score in the opposite goal. They retrieve the ball and run to join the other group.
Duration: Unspecified.

Alternatives:

- Play to a time limit.
- Perform a certain number of circuits.
- Each player completes 10 circuits (= 20 shots on goal).
- Who scores the most goals?

Reaction I

Emphasis: Reaction speed.
Equipment: Balls.
Set-up: 1 goal.
Implementation: The keeper stands with his back to the coach. The coach gives a signal to the keeper when he kicks the ball, at which point the keeper turns around and fends off the ball.
Duration: Unspecified.
Alternatives:

- Shoot from different positions (inside right, center, inside left).
- The coach shoots from the ground or from his hands.
- The shots are kicked from different distances.

Reaction II

Emphasis: Reactions and mobility.

Equipment: Balls.

Set-up: 1 goal.

Implementation: 5 players with a ball each stand spread out along the 10-yard line. On a signal from the coach (number or name), the named player shoots at the goal.

Duration: 5 shots = 1 series, perform several series.

Alternatives:

- Change positions continuously.
- Vary distances.
- Kick the ball from the ground.
- Kick the ball from the hand.

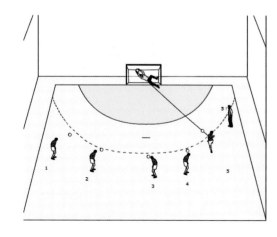

Target Throwing

Emphasis: Throwing accuracy.

Equipment: Balls, 5 cones.

Set-up: Half a pitch, goal on the center line.

Implementation: The coach throws or kicks a ball to the keeper, who then throws the ball accurately to hit a cone.

Duration: Unspecified.

Alternatives:

- Throw at the cones in order.
- Throw at the cones following the coach's instructions.
- Change the positions of the cones.
- Vary the distances to and between the cones.
- The keeper must throw to the left or right.
- With a forfeit: maximum of 10 attempts, for each miss the keeper does a push-up/sprint, for each hit the coach does.

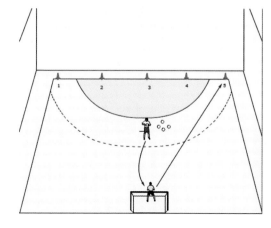

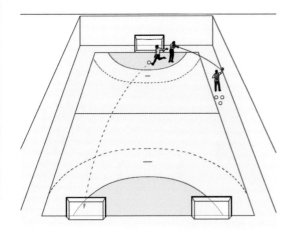

Goal Shooting

Emphasis: Shooting accuracy.

Equipment: Balls, portable goals (goal frames, cone goals, soft landing mats), depending on the available facilities.

Set-up: Whole pitch.

Implementation: The coach throws or kicks the ball to the keeper, who catches the ball and kicks it into a goal at the opposite end of the pitch.

Duration: Unspecified.

Alternatives:

- The keeper must alternate between kicking with the right and left feet.
- 10 attempts: for each miss the keeper performs a push-up/sprint, for each goal the coach does.

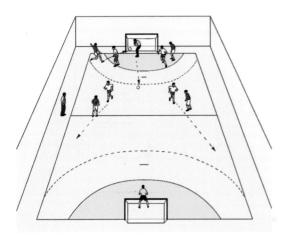

Goalkeeper as Attacker

Emphasis: Quick switch.

Equipment: Balls

Set-up: Whole pitch, players are divided into 2 groups.

Implementation: The keeper catches a ball kicked from the side and starts a fast attack with 2 teammates against 2 defenders + goalkeeper (situation: 3 v 2 + keeper). The other players may not attack. This is followed by an attack from the other side.

Duration: Unspecified.

Alternative: Each team has 10 attempts – who scores the most goals?

Uneven-sided Teams with Goalkeeper

Emphasis: Tactics, goalkeeper as fieldplayer.

Equipment: Balls, 2 goals, bibs.

Set-up: Whole pitch, divide players into 2 groups.

Implementation: All players in the attacking team stand in the opposing team's half, the keeper plays as a 5th player. If the keeper sees a chance to take a shot at the goal himself, he tries it. A teammate must then cover the center of the pitch and prevent a possible counterattack.

Duration: Unspecified.

Alternative:

- Each attack must be played via the goalkeeper.
- Every attack must include at least one ball contact by the keeper.

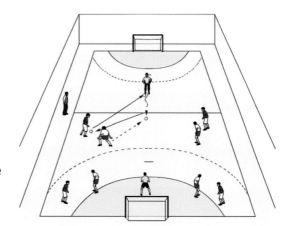

Ball Catcher

Emphasis: Fast reactions, conditioning.

Equipment: Balls, cones.

Set-up: Mark out 2 pitches of approx. 11 x 11 yards.

Implementation: 2 coaches/players throw the ball high into the air one after the other. The keeper catches it and throws it back.

Duration: Unspecified.

Alternatives:

- The keeper must catch kicked balls.
- The throws/kicks come from different distances and at different times.
- On the coach's command, the keepers swap the marked areas as quickly as possible.

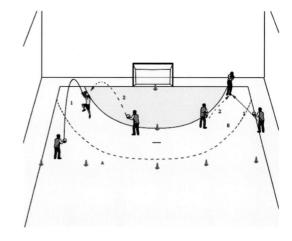

Scoring Spree

Emphasis: Goal defense

Equipment: Balls, 5 cones.

Set-up: Practice using 1 goal.

Implementation: The players shoot at the goal one after the other or after a signal from the coach. The keeper tries to deflect the balls. If he cannot catch the balls, he should deflect them to the side (not to the center).

Alternatives:

- Vary the sequence of the shots on goal.
- Vary the distances to the goal.
- For each 'clean' goal, the keeper does a push-up, or for each missed shot, the attacker does.
- The coach bets on the strikers or the keeper and must then join in with the respective forfeits.

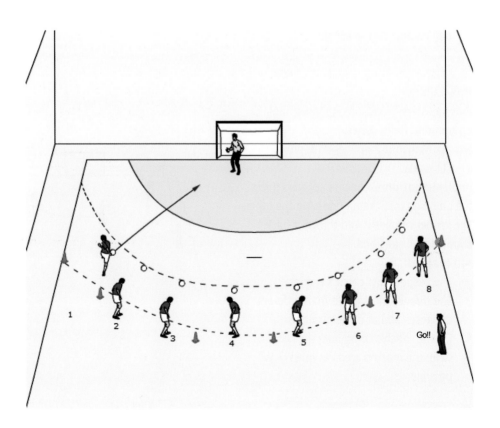

6

6 Organizational Tips

6.1 Organizational tips for training

6.1.1 Planning a training session

Effective organization is essential for a successful training session in which players achieve their learning objectives. The coach must therefore take the following conditions into account when planning the training session.

How big is the hall?
Make use of dividers like long benches or partitions in order to make the best use of a hall and to allow several groups to train at the same time. Cones, corner flags and markings on the hall floor are also useful as visual space dividers as they correspond to Futsal's nature, i.e. a game without walls. It is a way of creating additional versatile playing areas.

How many players are likely to take part in the training session?
This impacts on group formation; do I have alternative solutions for an odd and even number of players? Can the group be divided into two, three or four teams?

Which and how much equipment, balls etc. can I use?
This also includes equipment maintenance: are the balls pumped up, is equipment such as cones, bibs, posts etc. really available exactly as it was in previous training sessions?

What will be the emphasis of this training session?

What is the training condition of my players, what stage of the season are we at?

The coach should present the session as a discrete unit with a beginning and an end. This includes the coach arriving in the hall at least 15 minutes before his players so that he can welcome the players at the start and they can all begin the session together. Likewise, when the coach says goodbye, the session is over.

6.1.2 Organization forms in training

The circuit

The many and varied demands of Futsal, particularly where youngsters' training is concerned, can be really creatively and variably combined in carousel activities and circuits:

1. The versatility circuit offers a varied movement training with running, jumping, rolling, balancing, etc.

2. The technique circuit solicits different Futsal techniques like dribbling, passing and shooting at the goal.

3. The combi circuit includes movement tasks from different areas that can be combined in a varied and interesting way.

Circuits can be divided into two basic organizational forms:

1. In the *individual* circuit, the players must be distributed evenly around the stations at the start to avoid unnecessary waiting time. The sizes of the groups determine the length of the circuit and the number of activities. However, if the line waiting at some stations gets too long, other stations or parallel circuits must be set up.

2. Equally-sized groups complete the circuit in teams in the group *circuit.* Here the motivation-boosting aspect of competition between the groups comes into play. The fact that even large groups can all train at the same time in small spaces (and with little equipment) is an added bonus.

When coaching youngsters, the coach should demonstrate the circuit once himself as children find it easier to copy something they have seen rather than just to follow verbal instructions.

If there are big differences in performance ability within a training group, it is a good idea to use group circuits that are set up according to performance and ability levels (also in parallel).

Circuits enable the coach to keep an eye on each child at once. All children start at the same time, and the coach can help specific children if he spots a problem.

In competitions, the announcing of intermediate results motivates the groups.

The gap

The gap form is particularly suitable for technique training. The gap guarantees frequent ball contact and multiple repetitions, enabling basic techniques like passing, ball reception or lobs to be practiced effectively. Stop technique drills from being monotonous though by incorporating game forms or competitions to liven things up.

Nearly every drill can also be performed as a competition, e.g. between 2 groups.

You can also add variety by incorporating extra movements, e.g. partners swap places or the whole gap turns in one direction thus forming new drill pairings.

Even for larger groups, the gap form guarantees the coach a good overview and enables him to correct individual players where necessary.

Goal scoring training

Goal scoring training should definitely be included in every Futsal training session starting at a very young age, as scoring goals is highly motivating. The drills should therefore always be set up to allow many goals to be scored (wide goals, many repetitions, favorable distance to the goal, etc.).

To keep the pace of the drill high, the goals should be set up in front of a wall so that the ball does not roll away, can be retrieved immediately and does not get in the way of other groups.

For goal scoring training, which is already very demanding in itself, small contests add to the competitive atmosphere.

In general, bear in mind that especially in Junior Futsal, varied, playful, fun and age-appropriate drills and game forms should be offered. They are highly motivating and support performance development.

Every drill and game form should be organized so that plenty of action and short waiting times are guaranteed for every single player!

6.2 Organizational tips for match day

Along with organizational pre-planning of training sessions, the actual match day must also be planned in detail. The coach has specific duties before match day, during the match and a debrief with constructive criticism after the match.

6.2.1 The coach's duties before the game

If it is a home game, the sports hall must be booked in time. A site visit gives an idea of whether the selected hall is suitable to hold a Futsal match. Are appropriate floor markings in place? Is there a big enough space between the side and goal lines to the walls or stands? Are handball goals available? Does the club/team have the "power of the keys" so that there is greater flexibility regarding playing times? Is it possible to sell food and drink as a potential way of filling the club's coffers? To WHOM can I delegate WHICH tasks? WHO is bringing WHAT?

For the team journey to an away game, a precise meeting point must be agreed. The approximate traveling time to the match venue should be calculated. Depending on how long it is, an adequate time buffer should be allowed. A list of the cell phone numbers of all players should be available to be able to check up on those who are late and enable a flexible response.

Are all the essentials good to go? First aid kit, set of jerseys, bibs for substituted players, players' licenses? Here too the same questions should be asked: WHO is bringing WHAT? To WHOM can I delegate WHAT?

Once these details are taken care of, the coach can concentrate on the upcoming game. In order to be able to prepare his team optimally to face the next opponent, the coach must familiarize himself with them, have analyzed their strengths and weaknesses and have up-to-date information on them. Knowledge of all these factors will allow him to determine his team's lineup. Prior to that, in the medium term he should enquire as to which players are actually available on the date of the game in order to be able also to structure training according to the composition of the team.

If the squad is very big, it may not be necessary for all players to attend the match, unless they are going to support their team. This must also be explained in order to avoid possible disappointment (particularly in the case of young players), if it is likely that a player will not be taking part in the match.

The pre-planning of the game proceeds from these parameters:

- What will the starting lineup be?
- Which tactics will be used against the upcoming opponent?
- Which substitutions or tactical adjustments are envisaged?
- Which final advice will be given to the team before the game?

While the team gets changed, the coach has the opportunity to get an impression of the sports hall. Are there any special features worth noting, what is the lighting like, are there recommendations for the team captain regarding the choice of end?

Subsequently, he supports his team's warm-up program, talks personally to a few players and gives individual advice.

Directly before the kick-off, the final BRIEF tactical and/or motivational tips can be given. The players come to the circle together to demonstrate their unity as a team. A final 'battle cry' adds to the pre-start tension and allows the players to start the game concentrated and 'raring to go'.

6.2.2 The coach's duties during the game

During the game, the coach must make an analytical observation of both his and the opposing team:

- Is the previously discussed strategy implemented?
- Does the opposing team largely let this happen or must the coach react immediately with an alternative tactic?
- Are all players in the expected shape or are shortcomings already noticeable in the starting phase of the match?

By means of the 'flying change' that is possible in Futsal, the coach can react very quickly to game situations and put the most appropriate players on the pitch.

If the coach intervenes verbally in the game, it must be in a calm and objective way. The instructions must be brief, clear and unambiguous. They should be directed at specific players as far as possible; random shouting and general remarks do not have a positive effect on the course of the game. An agitated commentary on every scene is counterproductive and not helpful for the players.

At half-time, drinks are provided and it is the first opportunity for recovery. It is not a good idea to talk directly to the players, and likewise general discussions of mistakes or the expression of personal opinions by players should be banned by the coach.

The coach should analyze the first half succinctly and clearly and formulate consequences for the team. Positive, specific and forward-looking instructions are most effective.

A rousing cheer to create new excitement and a new sense of unity for the second half then ends the half-time break.

6.2.3 The coach's duties after the game

Depending on the outcome of the match, the coach can either celebrate with his team or provide the necessary consolation. In the case of a victory, the coach can praise the team as a whole but also give generous individual praise, without leaving any players out.

In the case of a defeat, direct negative criticism should be avoided – the team has already been punished enough!

It is absolutely inadmissible to punish individual players by singling out their individual mistakes in front of the whole team. While this may temporarily allow the coach to let off steam, it is not pedagogically sound and definitely not conducive to the development of the psychological strength of the players. That does not mean that no mistakes may be discussed, but this should be done objectively and in a relaxed atmosphere with the necessary distance from the previous match day.

The coach can look to the future by focusing on the following week's training and announce emphases based on his updated knowledge.

In the next training session he can then hold individual discussions and also express individual criticisms, but always with the intention of correcting mistakes and encouraging the player(s) concerned. A communal analysis of the last match day helps to uncover errors and highlight strengths.

From his personal and accumulated findings, the coach can draw conclusions for future training planning: must the emphases in training be shifted? Do any players require special technique training? Was the team able to implement the desired tactics?

By means of analysis, the coach can further optimize his training program and ensure his team's ongoing improvement. The many different factors that make up a team's success or failure should be considered. A good coach is familiar with these factors; he guides, leads and helps where important and appropriate.

7   Abridged Rules

**FIFA Futsal Laws of the Game 2008
(Extracts)**

References to the male gender in the Futsal Laws of the Game in respect of referees, players and officials are for simplification and apply to both males and females.

1 – THE PITCH

Dimensions
The pitch shall be rectangular. The length of the touch line shall be greater than the length of the goal line.
Length: minimum 25 m, maximum 42 m
Width: minimum 15 m, maximum 25 m

The pitch and its features are shown in the following diagram:

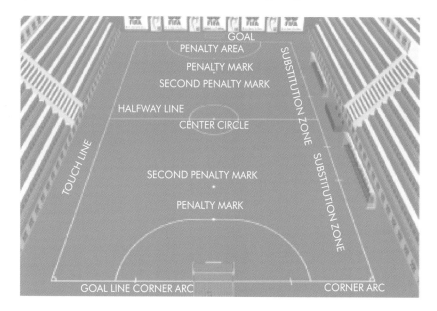

The penalty mark
A mark shall be drawn 6 m from the midpoint between the goalposts and equidistant from them.

The second penalty mark
A second mark shall be drawn on the pitch 10 m from the midpoint between the goalposts and equidistant from them.

Substitution zones
The substitution zones are the areas on the touch line in front of the team benches that the players shall use to enter and leave the pitch.

The goals

The distance (inside measurement) between the posts shall be 3 m (3.3 yd) and the distance from the lower edge of the crossbar to the ground shall be 2 m (2.2 yd).

Safety

The goals shall have a stabilizing system that prevents them from overturning. Portable goals may be used provided that they are as stable as normal goals.

2 – THE BALL

Qualities and measurements

The ball shall be:
- spherical
- made of leather or another suitable material
- of a circumference of not less than 62 cm and not more than 64 cm
- not less than 400 grams nor more than 440 grams in weight at the start of the match
- of a pressure equal to 0. 4-0.6 atmospheres (400-600 g/cm^2) at sea level.

3 – THE NUMBER OF PLAYERS

Players

A match shall be played by two teams, each consisting of no more than five players, one of whom is the goalkeeper.

Substitution procedure

Substitutes may be used in any match that is part of an official competition organized by FIFA, a confederation or a member association.

The maximum number of substitutes permitted is seven. The number of substitutions that may be made during a match is unlimited.

A player who has been replaced may return to the pitch as a substitute for another player. A substitution may be made at any time, regardless of whether the ball is in play or not, provided that the following conditions are observed:
- The player leaving the pitch does so via his own team's substitution zone.

- The player entering the pitch does so via his own team's substitution zone but not until the player leaving the pitch has completely crossed the touch line.
- A goalkeeper may change places with any other player.

Decisions

1 *At the start of a match, each team shall have five players.*
2 *If, in the event of players being sent off, fewer than three players (including the goalkeeper) are left in either of the teams, the match shall be abandoned.*
3 *A team official may give tactical instructions to players during a match. However, team officials shall not obstruct players and referees, placing themselves within the technical area, where one exists, and shall always behave in an appropriate manner.*

4 – THE PLAYERS' EQUIPMENT

Safety

A player shall not use equipment or wear anything (including any kind of jewelry) that could be dangerous to himself or another player.

Basic equipment

The basic compulsory equipment of a player comprises the following separate articles:

- A jersey or shirt with sleeves – if undergarments are worn, the color of the sleeve must be of the same main color as the sleeve of the jersey or shirt
- Shorts – if undershorts are worn, they must be of the same main color as the shorts
- Socks
- Shinguards
- Footwear – the only types of footwear permitted are canvas or soft-leather training or gymnastic shoes with soles of rubber or a similar material.

Shinguards

- Shall be entirely covered by the socks
- Shall be made of a suitable material (rubber, plastic or similar substances)
- Shall provide a reasonable degree of protection.

Goalkeepers
- The goalkeeper is permitted to wear long trousers.
- Each goalkeeper shall wear colors that easily distinguish him from the other players and the referees.
- If an outfield player replaces a goalkeeper, he shall wear a goalkeeper's jersey with his number marked on the back.

5-6– THE REFEREE

Each match shall be controlled by two referees, who have full authority to enforce the Laws of the Game in connection with the match to which they have been appointed.

The second referee shall operate on the opposite side of the pitch to the referee and shall also be equipped with a whistle.

A timekeeper and third referee shall be appointed. They shall be positioned off the pitch, level with the halfway line. They shall be equipped with a suitable clock (chrono-meter) and the necessary equipment to keep a record of accumulated fouls.

7 – THE DURATION OF THE MATCH

Periods of play
The match shall last two equal periods of 20 minutes.

Time-out
The teams are entitled to a one-minute time-out in each half.

A time-out may be requested at any time but is permitted only when the team requesting the time-out is in possession of the ball.

General
All play must be resumed within 4 seconds otherwise the referee will give possession of the ball to the opposing team. Exceptions to this rule are the kick-off and penalty kick, when the referee's whistle must be awaited.

11 – FOULS AND MISCONDUCT

Fouls and misconduct shall be penalized as follows:

Direct free kick

A direct free kick shall be awarded to the opposing team if a player commits any of the following seven infringements in a manner considered by the referees to be careless, reckless or excessively forceful:
- kicking or attempting to kick an opponent
- tripping or attempting to trip an opponent, either by sliding or by bending down in front of or behind him,
- jumping on an opponent
- charging an opponent
- striking or attempting to strike an opponent
- tackling an opponent
- pushing an opponent

A direct free kick shall also be awarded to the opposing team if a player commits any of the following four infringements:
- holding an opponent
- spitting at an opponent
- sliding in an attempt to play the ball while an opponent is playing it or is about to play it (sliding tackle), except for the goalkeeper in his own penalty area, provided that he does not endanger the safety of an opponent
- carrying, striking or throwing the ball with one's hands or arms, except for the goalkeeper in his own penalty area

The direct free kick shall be taken from the place where the infringement occurred, unless the free kick has been awarded to the defending team in its own penalty area, in which case the free kick may be taken from any point inside the penalty area.

The above-mentioned infringements are accumulated fouls.

Penalty kick

A penalty kick shall be awarded if a player commits any of the aforementioned infringements inside his own penalty area, irrespective of the position of the ball but provided that it is in play.

Indirect free kick

An indirect free kick shall be awarded to the opposing team if a goalkeeper commits any of the following offences:

- after clearing the ball, he touches it again following a deliberate pass by a team-mate, before it has crossed the halfway line or been played or touched by an opponent
- he touches or controls the ball with his hands after it has been deliberately kicked to him by a team-mate
- he touches or controls the ball with his hands after he has received it directly from a kick-in taken by a team-mate
- he touches or controls the ball with his hands or feet in his own half for more than four seconds.

An indirect free kick shall also be awarded to the opposing team from the place where the infringement occurred, if, in the opinion of the referee, a player:

- plays in a dangerous manner
- deliberately obstructs an opponent
- prevents the goalkeeper from throwing the ball with his hands
- commits any other infringement not previously mentioned in Law 11 for which play is stopped to caution or dismiss a player.

The indirect free kick shall be taken from the place where the infringement occurred.

Cautionable offences

A player shall be cautioned if he commits any of the following infringements:

- unsporting behavior
- dissent by word or action
- persistent infringement of the Futsal Laws of the Game
- delaying the restart of play
- failure to respect the required distance when play is restarted with a corner kick, kick-in, free kick or goal clearance
- entering or re-entering the pitch without the referees' permission or infringement of the substitution procedure
- deliberately leaving the pitch without the referees' permission

A substitute shall be cautioned if he commits any of the following infringements:

- unsporting behavior

- dissent by word or action
- delaying the restart of play

Sending-off offences
A player or a substitute shall be sent off if he commits any of the following offences:
- serious foul play
- violent conduct
- spitting at an opponent or any other person
- denying the opposing team a goal or an obvious goalscoring opportunity by deliberately handling the ball (with the exception of a goalkeeper inside his own penalty area)
- denying an opponent moving towards the player's goal an obvious goalscoring opportunity by committing an offence punishable by a free kick or a penalty kick
- using offensive, insulting or abusive language or gestures
- receiving a second caution in the same match

A substitute shall be sent off if he commits the following offence:
- denying the opposing team a goal or an obvious goalscoring opportunity

Decisions
A player who has been sent off may not re-enter the play.
A substitute player may enter the pitch two full minutes after a team-mate has been sent off, unless a goal is scored before the two minutes have elapsed, and provided he has the authorization of the timekeeper.
A tackle that endangers the safety of an opponent shall be sanctioned as serious foul play.
Any act of simulation on the pitch that is intended to deceive the referees shall be sanctioned as unsporting behavior.

13 – ACCUMULATED FOULS

Accumulated fouls
- are those punished by a direct free kick as mentioned in Law 11.
- the first 5 accumulated fouls committed by each team during each half are recorded in the match report.

- the referees may allow play to continue by applying the advantage rule if the team has not yet committed 5 accumulated fouls and the opposing team is not denied an obvious goalscoring opportunity.
- when applying the advantage rule, the referees shall use the mandatory signal to indicate an accumulated foul to the timekeeper and the third referee as soon as the ball is out of play.
- if extra time is played, accumulated fouls from the second period shall remain valid. Any accumulated fouls during extra time shall be added to the team's total from the second period.

Position of free kick

For the first five accumulated fouls recorded against either team in each half, and provided the game has been stopped for that reason:

- the players of the opposing team may form a wall to defend a free kick
- all opponents shall be situated at least 5 m from the ball
- a goal may be scored directly in the opponents' goal from this free kick.

Beginning with the sixth accumulated foul recorded against either team in each half:

- the defending team's players may not form a wall to defend a free kick
- the player taking the kick shall be duly nominated
- the goalkeeper shall remain in his penalty area at a distance of at least 5 m from the ball
- all the other players shall remain on the pitch behind an imaginary line that is level with the ball and parallel to the goal line, and outside the penalty area. They

shallremain 5 m away from the ball and may not obstruct the player taking the free kick.

No player may cross this imaginary line until the ball has been struck and starts to move.

Procedure (for the sixth and any subsequent accumulated fouls)

- the player taking the free kick shall kick the ball with the intention of scoring a goal and may not pass the ball to a team-mate.
- once the free kick has been taken, no player may touch the ball until it has been touched by the defending goalkeeper, rebounded off the goalpost or crossbar, or left the pitch.
- additional time shall be allowed for a direct free kick to be taken at the end of each half or at the end of each period of extra time.

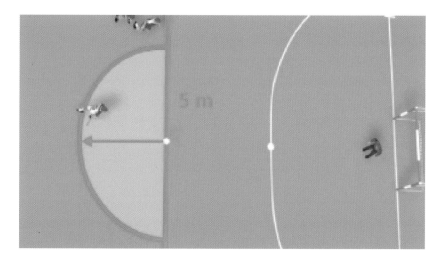

14 – THE PENALTY KICK

A penalty kick is awarded against a team that commits any of the infringements for which a direct free kick is awarded inside its own penalty area and while the ball is in play.

A goal may be scored directly from a penalty kick.

Additional time shall be allowed for a penalty kick to be taken at the end of each half or at the end of each period of extra time.

15 – THE KICK-IN

The kick-in is a method of restarting play.

A goal may not be scored directly from a kick-in.

A kick-in:

- shall be awarded when the whole of the ball crosses the touch line, either along the ground or through the air, or hits the ceiling
- shall be taken from the place where the ball crossed the touch line
- shall be awarded to the opponents of the player who last touched the ball.

Position of the ball and the players

The ball:

- shall remain stationary on the touch line
- may be kicked back onto the pitch in any direction

The player taking the kick-in:

- shall have part of one foot on the touch line or off the pitch at the moment he takes the kick-in.

The players of the defending team:

- shall be at least 5 m from the place where the kick-in is taken

Procedure

- the player taking the kick-in shall do so within four seconds of receiving the ball.
- the player taking the kick-in may not play the ball a second time until it has touched another player.
- the ball shall be deemed in play as soon as it enters the pitch.

16 – THE GOAL CLEARANCE

The goal clearance

The goal clearance is a method of restarting play.

A goal may not be scored directly from a goal clearance.

A goal clearance shall be awarded when:

- the whole of the ball, having last touched a player of the attacking team, crosses the goal line either along the ground or through the air, and a goal is not scored.

Procedure

- the ball shall be thrown from any point inside the penalty area by the goalkeeper.
- opponents shall remain outside the penalty area until the ball is in play.
- the goalkeeper may not play the ball a second time until it has been touched by an opponent or is returned to him by a teammate once it has crossed the halfway line.

REFEREE SIGNALS

Start and restart of play (kick-off) (photo a)

Direct free kick/penalty kick (photo b)

Indirect free kick (photo c)

Corner kick (photo d)

Kick-in (photo e)

Four second count (photo f)

Fifth accumulated foul (photo g)

Advantage accumulated foul (photo h)

Advantage indirect foul (photo i)

Accumulated foul (photos j + k)

Caution (photo l)

Sending-off (photo m)

Time-out (photo n)

8   Contact addresses

FIFA

FIFA House, 11 Hitzigweg
8030 Zurich
Switzerland
Telefon: 41-1/3849595,
Telefax: 41-1/3849696
Internet: www. fifa. com

UEFA

Route de Genéve 46
Case postale
CH-1260 Nylon 2
Switzerland
Telefon: 41-22/9944444
Telefax: 41-22/9944488
Internet: www. uefa. com
E-Mail: info@uefa. com

Bibliography

Brüggemann, Detlev (1999). *Kinder- und Jugendtraining.* Schorndorf.

Burns, Tim (2004). *Holistic futsal.* Lulu Pr.

de Silva, Ricardo & Filho, Clovis (2005). *Technique and tactics.* FIFA. Zürich.

DFB-Training online. www. dfb. de.

Engler, Rainer & von Coelln, Georg (2007). *Futsal – Ein Ball geht seinen Weg.* Eine Informationsschrift des Westdeutschen Fußball- und Leichtathletikverbandes e. V. Duisburg.

FIFA (2008). *Futsal-Spielregeln* 2008. Zürich.

Frick, Ulrich & Heim, Christopher (2006c). *Futsal in der Schule – neue Erkenntnisse zum Einfluss des Ballmaterials bei der Fußballvermittlung an Schülerinnen und Schüler der Klasse 6.* In: Raab, Markus et al. (Hrsg.). Zukunft der Sportspiele: fördern, fordern, forschen. Flensburg University Press, Flensburg. 73-77.

Hoek, Jan & Boer, Gert (1986). *Zaalvoetbal.* Haarlem.

Kammerer, Stephan & Engler, Rainer (2008) *Futsal: Das offizielle FIFA-Futsal-Regelwerk mit Kommentaren und Hintergründen.* Aachen.

Lozano, Javier & Hermans, Vic (2003). *Futsal-Trainer.* FIFA. Zürich.

Peter, Ralf & Bode, Gerd (2005). *Fußball von morgen, Kinderfußball.* Offizielles Lehrbuch des DFB. Münster.

Stritz, Michal (2002). *Technicko-Taktické Zkusenosti.* Vydava.

Teunissen, Evert (1988). *Zaalvoetbal.* Baarn.

Photo Credits

Interior photos: Nils Eden, Dortmund (Germany)
Nicole Gdawietz, Mülheim an der Ruhr (Germany)
Jessica Förster, Moers (Germany)
Georg von Coelln, Münster (Germany)

The graphics were produced with "easy Sports-Graphics" (www. sportgrafiken. de).

Graphics in chapter 7: FIFA

Jacket photo: dpa Picture Alliance; © Fotolia.com
Jacket design: Sabine Groten

Acknowledgements

Thank you to the players Zaid el Morabiti and Pieter Grimmelins for making themselves available for the technique photos in Chapter 3.

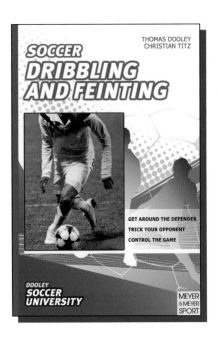

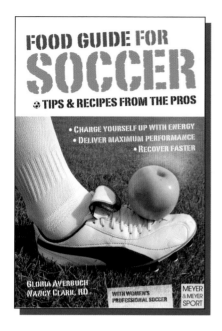
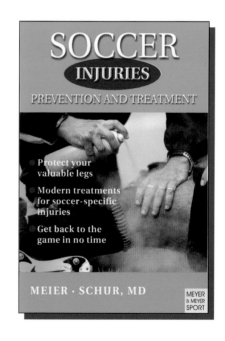